Shares without Tears

The Private Investor's Guide to Share Trading

Jennie Hawthorne

TTL is an imprint of
Take That Ltd.
P.O.Box 200,
Harrogate
HG1 2YR
ENGLAND

email:sales@takethat.co.uk

www.takethat.co.uk

ISBN: 1-903994-00-4

10 9 8 7 6 5 4 3 2 1

Trademarks:
Trademarked names are used throughout this book. Rather than place a trademark symbol in every occurance of a trademark name, the names are being used only in an editorial fashion for the benefit of the trademark owner, with no intention to infringe the trademark.

Printed and bound in The United Kingdom.

Disclaimer:
The information in this publication is distributed on an "as is" basis, without warranty. While very effort has been made to ensure that this book is free from errors or omissions, neither the author, the publisher, or their respective employees and agents, shall have any liability to any person or entity with respect to any liability, loss or damage caused or alleged to have been caused directly or indirectly by advice or instructions contained in this book or by the computer hardware or software products described herein. **Readers are urged to seek prior expert advice before making decisions, or refraining from making decisions, based on information or advice contained in this book.**

TTL books are available at special quantity discounts to use as premiums and sales promotions. For more information, please contact the Director of Special Sales at the above address or contact your local bookshop.

Contents

Acknowledgements

...and thanks to:

- my parents Jim and Susan Crawley for their example of survival in a harsh climate;
- the staff of St. Anne's School, Whitechapel, London, E1, for illustrating the value of education;
- the teachers at Notre Dame High School, Southwark, who strove valiantly,with limited success, to change a sow's ear into a silk purse;
- former colleagues at South West London College, many now distinguished figures in politics and universities, for so freely passing on their expertise;
- friends in the press and financial institutions who helped me on my way;

And finally but never least to Frank, husband, friend and partner, for his investment knowledge and **The Last Word** in this book and to our children: Michael, computer buff, incredibly patient and helpful with his less IT-literate mother; Stephanie for her journalistic expertise; Francine for her encyclopaedic knowledge of who reads what; Jennifer for her imagination; Jeremy for his generosity; Kathy of Hatricks with her PR skills and John for his unfailing good humour, no matter what the stock markets say.

Chapter 1

Finding the cash

"One of the virtues of being very young is that you
don't let the facts get in the way of your imagination."
Sam Levinson

Reasons for investing

WHY INVEST in shares? The answer is simple: investment, done correctly, gets a higher return than the miserable one or two per cent you receive for the use of your money elsewhere.

Unlike the setting up of your own business or acquiring other assets such as property, you need no loans, no equipment (other than perhaps a PC or calculator) and very little capital to buy a few shares in UK or US companies. Over the long term, they have consistently outperformed building society, bank and other forms of deposit accounts. This is the main purpose of investment: to make money grow more and faster than it would do anywhere else.

It is just an efficient way of creating a modicum of wealth. There is nothing greedy or immoral about this. If you wish, you can give all your gains away to good causes, family or friends. Make your pile, gobble it all up and enjoy your fill or join the philanthropists who distribute some of their wealth to those less fortunate than themselves. The choice is yours. But first you have to create the wealth. So, how do you start?

Finding the cash

To buy shares, you must enter the stock market and offer cash for your purchase. Cash! Where is that coming from when you have a load of debt weighing like a millstone round your neck? But there is no use dreaming about making millions as an investor, with a stretch limo in the drive, and properties in all the most desirable areas of the world, if you cannot pay the bills. All kinds of horrors from loss of home or goods to prison and bankruptcy lie in wait for those who spend what they haven't got, cannot make repayments on what they have borrowed, and ignore the 'Dear Sir, unless…' type of letter.

Only seasoned investors can buy or sell shares without any cash, on margin, as it is euphemistically known. Having 'bought' shares in this way at a low price, they hope the share price will rise. If it does, they 'sell' the shares and pocket the profit between the buying and selling prices. Or again with no upfront cash, they 'sell' shares at a high price, and hope the price falls so that they can 'buy' back, at this lower price the shares which they have already 'sold'. This tactic also makes a profit with no start-up cash.

It is not as easy as it looks. Suppose Alan 'buys' shares on margin. The cost is $1000 which has to be paid by the settlement date. Before that day comes, the price has already fallen to $500. Has Alan the nerve to hold on? He has. But the bouncing ball of the share price has not yet touched the ground. Alan must sell…but cannot get ahead of the other bears heading for the exit. He licks his wounds and takes a big loss.

Transactions like these are, to misquote Stevie Smith's poem, not investing but trading. Trading is short term, and more widely practised in America where, with only around $2000 in your account, you can buy shares costing double.

Borrowing for share purchase like this is not so easy unless you have an account with one of the financial or sporting bookmakers. They quote prices for individual shares, global stock markets, FTSE, Dow, etc., and more esoteric choices such as options and currencies. Prices have a little extra added on. This 'spread' is also added to or deducted from share prices when you buy or sell through a broker in the stock market. For illustrative purposes only, an example of financial spread betting is given below.

Example: Financial spread betting

You buy ABC shares costing 173–176p (note the spread of 3p) at say £10 per point. This means that for every penny rise in the share you 'win' £10, for every penny downturn you lose £10 – a highly risky and dramatic form of share trading, though you could choose more or less than £10 per point.

The price of ABC shares rises to 196–199p. You sell at 196p. Your profit on the deal is 196p - 176p x £10, that is 20 x £10 = £200.

Don't be deluded. You could lose as much and more quickly. The reality is that this is gambling, not investing. Take it up when you are sitting pretty on a cushion of accumulated wealth and can easily afford to lose your shirt, or cannot resist the thrill of the chase. To invest in shares, you almost always need cash, yours or another's.

From debt to credit

Cash is not so easy to find in the twenty-first century, when debt is a fact of life. Student loans, mortgages, credit and debit cards, hire purchase payments, maintenance for spouse/child 1/2/3…. How do you get rid of this incubus and create the cash to invest in shares?

One man who worked for 40 years on a pittance, was asked how he was able to retire to a grand house in the country with an income of £50,000 a year. His answer, "Hard work," mystified everybody until he added, "It also helps to have a rich relation who leaves you a couple of million when he dies."

If you lack a wealthy and doting relative at death's door, there are other possibilities. You might hit the jackpot with a lottery win, or strike it rich by marrying a millionaire, (more chancy still, unless you are a foreign beauty tying in your lot with a doddering duke) or by being a handsome young hunk acting as a toyboy for a falling star afraid of coming down to earth.

Cost control

As such eventualities are unlikely to arise, aim for cost control. According to the American Express Bank, men often borrow upwards of £10,000 a time to stock up on status symbols and indulge in life's 'little luxuries'. In the UK this amounts to half the average salary for men aged 21–49 years old. Young men particularly, view items like convertible cars, and high-tech gadgets as the latest 'must haves' and prefer personal loans for these purchases, leaving savings, if any, for holidays, essentials and emergencies.

Budgeting

Big spending gives no leeway for investing in shares, so make a budget and stick to it. Look at outgoings. Can any be reduced, perhaps with greater benefits to your health? Save a minimum of your salary, say at least 5% of your income, regularly. Push the percentage up to a monthly 12% as your wages rise. Get free credit by paying your bills within the time limit (around six weeks). Use a system of priorities. Change the dearest credit cards for cheaper ones. Start clearing off the cards that charge the highest interest rate. Pay more than the minimum monthly amount due. The following example shows why.

Example: Case history on borrowing

Ned has a credit card on which he carries over £1,000 a month. He pays off the minimum 5% each month and maintains his £1,000 balance. At the end of the year, Ned has paid interest on that £1,000 of £183.24 or 18.3% and still has the outstanding debt.

Ned would have to search for a very long time to find any savings plan that guaranteed him a yearly 18.3% interest. Before he can ever think of stock market investment he must somehow pay off the amount owed on his credit card and cut it up until he has managed to accumulate some savings. If ever Ned needs to borrow again, he wants to make sure he gets the right loan.

The right loan

With any borrowing (in any currency) it is essential to know how the length of a loan and the annual interest rate affect the monthly payment and total charges. Suppose Ned aims to save money, not spend it, but has to borrow $7500 for some absolutely essential purpose. He gets three quotes.

- a three year loan at an annual rate of 18%
- a two year loan also at 18%
- a two year loan at an annual rate of 16%

The monthly and total repayments are shown in the table below for loans 1, 2 and 3. Getting the quotes tells Ned what system will suit him best and what he has to pay to get it. A shorter lending period means cheaper monthly loans but a higher overall sum in total.

Loan for $7500 paid at 16% and 18% over two and three years				
	Period of loan: years	Annual rate:%	Monthly repayments	Total monthly repayment	Total repayment (+$7500)
Loan 1	3	18	$271.15	$2261.25	$9761.25
Loan 2	2	18	$374.44	$1486.50	$8986.59
Loan 3	2	16	$367. 22.	£1313.25.	$8813.25

Cost control and budgeting are tough disciplines. Over time they work. The phases of life when money flows out more quickly than it comes in disappear. Students get their first jobs, the big spender finds cheaper credit, wages and salaries go up a little, failed businesses rise again although not always with the same heads, mortgage outgoings appear less of a burden or, like other loans, get paid off. At last there is money to spare. How to spend it? Charitable giving? And afterwards…?

Regular saving

Set aside some cash for the inevitable rainy day, some to meet future needs, and arrange, as soon as you can for a pension at retirement. A very rough guide to get half your current salary, at a retirement age of 65, is to divide your current age by two and save that proportion of your salary every year. To be young and poor is bad; to be old and poor is worse.

To retire early means making bigger savings than if you give up work at the usual State retirement age. An occupational pension, provided by your firm, of say, two-thirds of your salary which you might expect then, is likely to be less than half that amount if you retire ten years earlier.

Examples: Saving for a pension – a 'rule of thumb' calculation

Julia Johnson is 24, single, earning £18,000 a year. She divides her age by two. Using the resultant figure of 12 means she must save £18,000/12 or £1500 a year to get half her present salary at retirement.

Jack Piper is 28. He earns £24,000 a year. To get half his current pay at retirement. he must save £24,000/14 or £1714 a year.

Pension schemes

Take up any concessions offered by employer or state, usually on tax, for pension and other saving. In the US there is the Individual Retirement Scheme, in the UK personal, stakeholder and self-invested personal pensions as well as the Individual Savings Account (ISA).

Unlike pension schemes, which give tax relief on the amount contributed, ISAs get relief on the savings themselves. Thus a subscription of a nominal £10 to a pension scheme, gives a tax concession relative to your age, so that you pay perhaps only £6 or less for £10 of benefit. But when you take the total out, it is taxed at whatever is the rate for your age and income. By contrast, £10 saved in an ISA means you have to put in the full £10 but when you withdraw it, as you can at any time, income and capital growth are tax-free.

In the UK, the stakeholder pension is a useful way of saving for a wife/partner who does not work outside the home. Unlike an investment in shares, or other type of saving, pensions cannot however be touched until the holder is of pensionable age. This is both the discipline and disadvantage of most pension schemes. Having arranged your pension, where should other savings be kept?

The examples given in Saving for a Pension illustrate two important truths, both well known but not always understood: time is money and time builds wealth. Wealth does not come from saving alone. Saving is passive, inactive, with little or no risk. You are merely lending your money to a financial institution which pays you a very small amount or nothing at all for its use.

Investment is by no means risk free but offers higher rewards. You could make 20% a year, double or triple your money over the long term. Take the wrong path and you could lose a lot. There is no compensation for share crashes, but anybody who does not know or care about stock market investment, and prefers to keep all their cash in the bank or building society, might change their minds after considering the following salutary examples:

Example: Saving without interest

John is 18 years old. With a gift of £100 he opens a bank current account. He receives a cheque book, a credit card if he wants one, and access to an Automatic Teller Machine (ATM...cash machine) which gives him immediate access to his money when he needs it.

The current account, providing these services, offers John no interest on his saving. In ten years, if he has not moved his money elsewhere, his £100 will still be safely resting in the bank. Depending on price rises over the ten years, it may be worth only half its original value.

Example: Saving with simple interest withdrawn

Ed and Mary Fuller are pensioners aged 65. Their savings of £10,000 earn 3% yearly interest. They want to keep their capital intact for when they are older, while using the annual £300 interest for holiday spending. At the end of 10 years, they still have their £10,000 in the bank, but have not allowed for the effects of inflation on their capital.

The purchasing power of their original £10,000, that is the amount of services and goods that it can buy, is now worth only £7374, a loss of £2626. If Ed and Mary want their £10,000 to keep its value for their later years, and are loath to invest in the stock market, they must forego the interest on their capital. Even then, if inflation rises above 3% the actual value of their original £10,000 will still show a loss.

Alternatively, if they cannot choose the investment route, they should open an account that operates the 'magic' of compound interest and withdraw none of it until needed when its 'magic' will be revealed.

Example: Saving; compound interest – no withdrawals

John and Jan have saved £10,000. They plan a wedding in two years with all the attendant frills and find an account paying 5% compound on their money. They do not touch the £500 interest paid yearly, so gain from the 'magic' of compound interest although this is only over a short period as follows:

Original Capital	*= £10,000*
Year 1: annual interest on £10,000 at 5%	*= £500*
Year 2: interest on £10,000 at 5%	*= £500*
Plus interest on Year 1's interest of £500	*= £25*
Capital (or principal) and interest at end of year 2	*= £11,125*

Inflation has made inroads on capital, but it is safe and worth more than it was when the account was opened. Compound interest mounts up over time. The Table below shows its effect over a period of up to 40 years which might include pension saving.

Future value of $1000 over a term of years: principal + accumulated interest						
	ANNUAL PERCENTAGE RATE					
Years	5%	6%	7%	8%	9%	10%
1	1050	1060	1070	1080	1090	1100
2	1103	1124	1145	1166	1188	1210
3	1158	1191	1225	1260	1295	1381
4	1216	1262	1311	1362	1412	1464
5	1276	1338	1403	1469	1539	1611
10	1710	1898	2105	2332	2580	2853
20	2653	3207	3870	4661	5604	6727
30	4322	5743	7612	10 063	13 268	17 449
40	7040	10 286	14 974	21 725	31 409	45 249

Source: *The Arithmetic of Interest Rates:* Federal Reserve Bank of New York.

The more frequent the intervals at which interest is calculated, the more rapidly interest builds up as this Table shows.

Interest rate	Frequency of interest payments if £1000 is invested for one year		
Per cent	Yearly	Quarterly	Monthly
3.5	1035.00	1035.46	1035.47
4.5	1045.00	1045.77	1045.94
5.5	1055.00	1056.14	1056.41
6.5	1065.00	1066.60	1066.97
7.5	1075.00	1077.14	1077.63

And daily compounding is better still.

Future value of $1000 over a term of years with daily compounding (360 day year)						
ANNUAL PERCENTAGE RATE						
Years	**5%**	**6%**	**7%**	**8%**	**9%**	**10%**
1	1052.0	1062.7	1073.5	10845	1095.5	1106.7
2	1106.7	1129.4	1152.5	11761	1200.2	1224.8
3	1164.2	1200.2	1246.7	12755	1314.8	1365.8
4	1224.8	1275.5	1328.2	13832	1095.5	1500.1
5	1288.5	1355.5	1425.9	15001	1578.1	1660.1
10	1660.2	1837.3	2033.3	22502	2490.3	2755.9
20	2756.1	3375.6	4134.3	50634	6201.4	7595.0
30	4575.6	6201.9	8406.1	113937	15443.0	20931.3

Source: *The Arithmetic of Interest Rates*: Federal Reserve Bank of New *York.*

Calculating compound interest

The formula for calculating compound interest is given below .

$$A = P \times (1 + R)^n$$

A equals the total amount received after investing an initial sum **P** (the Principal) at a given percentage interest rate, **R**, for a specified number of years, **n**.

If you have three of the four variables (amount, principal, rate and number of years), you can find out the fourth by varying the equation. As Albert Einstein is reputed to have said, "compounding interest is the greatest mathematical discovery of all time." The full power of compound interest relies on time and increases with time. $10,000 invested at 8% per year simple interest equals $34,000 at the end of 30 years. Compounded annually, it equals $100,627.

This 'mathematical discovery' can help you become a millionaire. With a monthly saving of $287 for 30 years invested in shares which yield over the period 12% compound, a not unattainable investment aim, you reach the million dollar mark of $1,003,054 by the end of the 30th. year. Over the 30 years, you actually save $103,320. The remaining $899,734 is interest plus interest on interest. That is the 'magic' of compound interest.

The Rule of 72

At 7 1/2% interest a sum of money will double itself in 10 years. A rough calculation sometimes known as the 'rule of 72' shows how long it takes, at a given interest rate, for any sum to double itself. You simply divide 72 by the rate of interest. As an example, take 7%, then 72/7 = 10.3, which means it will take roughly that number of years for £1000 to become approximately £2000.

Except in periods of very high inflation, you are unlikely ever to get 10% interest on bank or building society accounts... it can be as low as 2% but you would be very unlucky not to get a higher return on that from a five-year period of stock market investment. The contrast with savings accounts can be clearly seen in the following example.

Example: Investment in shares – no withdrawals

Due to retire in 1998, computer consultant John Edwards invests, in 1984, £10,000 in a group of UK shares. The dividends are reinvested. He also puts £1100 into a building society with a variable interest rate.

He lets this accumulate without drawing any interest. Thirteen years later, his £10,000 investment has grown to £83,284 while his £1100 building society savings have grown to just £1326 (sources: Barclays Equity index and UK Building Society index).

Even allowing for inflation and costs of commission, etc., on the shares this example highlights the difference between saving, even with compound interest, and investing in good quality shares. John might have chosen differently, but over time, good quality shares perform better than almost any other form of savings.

They solve the problem of how to make long-term money grow faster, and to keep savings ahead of inflation. For those who are still not convinced the next table shows the real annual returns of long-term equity investments in the US market over the past 70 years. Even during the leanest period 1971–80 equity investment shows a positive gain compared with bonds and cash.

Real annual average investment returns: %			
Decade	US stocks	US Bonds	US Cash
1931–1940	3.6	6.4	1.6
1941–1950	7.5	−3.1	−5.1
1951–1960	13.8	−0.4	−0.2
1961–1970	5.3	−1.5	1.3
1971–1980	1.4	−3.6	−1.1
1981–1990	7.9	8.8	3.9
1991–2000	14.1	7.1	1.9
Source: *The Economist, 5 May 2001.*			

Long term or short?

Some investors allege that the sure fire way to make money on the stock market is by moving in and out of it. It is certainly never wrong to take a profit and, if the chance arises, to move back when the market falls. However, Charles Schwab, founder of one of the world's largest stockbrokers commented on the difficulty of avoiding stock market falls by moving in and out. "I've never met anyone who has done it. Nor have I met anyone who knows someone who has done it." Brilliant investor and millionaire Warren Buffett adds, "If you are not prepared to hold an investment for ten years then do not hold it for ten minutes." Not everybody would be prepared to go along wholeheartedly with either comment but like most of Buffet's statements they contain a grain of truth.

Avoiding 'scams'

Having seen the 'magic' of compound interest and the need for long-term savings, take a look at what the stock market offers. Inspect the wares available there. Later chapters in this book tell how to assess, buy and sell them. That may stop you getting poorer but there is no guarantee that knowledge alone will make you rich. If it did, how would teachers and academics ever be recruited?

For the moment, be warned against 'scams' which lure people into a world of make-believe where fortunes are made by no effort, no talent and no cash. 'Junk' mail is one way of trading on this universal dream of becoming a millionaire. Bin it. Part with your money and you will get little, sometimes nothing, in return for your 'subscription.'

When an offer looks too good to be true, it generally is. Regard 'tips' about shares that are 'guaranteed' to go up in the next fortnight or month or whatever, with the same cynicism shown by Ralph Waldo Emerson when he said, "The more he mentioned his honour, the faster we counted our spoons."

Bulletin boards

Today's scams have a bigger net, and fatter fish to fry. Bulletin boards and chat forums on the Internet can be wonderful sources of information, but are sometimes used as bait to net suckers. 'Secret', or 'hot' information known only to the writer who may be using an alias, is given on the Net as to why this or that share is going to zoom. The 'advertiser' may well hold these shares himself. The price rises and enables him to sell at a profit. Rigorously check these tips. When in doubt, leave out.

Summary

Debt

- Avoid overdrafts, particularly 'unscheduled' ones. They cost an arm and a leg.
- Do not pay an annual fee for the use of a credit card. If you have to use one, make sure its interest rate charge is the lowest available.
- Prioritise debts. Government authorities (Revenue, Excise, etc.) are the most stringent in wanting their 'cut'. Pay them first, then those charging the highest interest rate.

Savings/investments

- You earn a fortune in a lifetime.
- Save a regular percentage each week/month: add up your yearly commitments, divide by 12 and use one-twelfth of cash savings (earning interest) to pay them.
- Get the best rate for your savings.
- Keep enough money for emergencies.
- Use your cash to bargain.
- Make personal pension provision to avoid too much reliance on state schemes.
- Having created some savings that in the short term you can afford to lose, think about long-term investing in shares.

Chapter 2

Creating a personal portfolio

I remember an occasion, early in my career, when I was
practically wiped out in my personal account.
George Soros

Sharing in another's fortune

INVESTMENT IN anything means putting time and/or money into the operation. When you have enough spare cash, from savings, windfall, legacy, insurance policy or whatever, it is then possible to start investing. You can invest directly by setting up your own business. In this case you might become a millionaire entrepreneur like Bill Gates of Microsoft, or Richard Branson of Virgin or Anita Roddick of Body Shop... or you can make your money grow indirectly by sharing in the businesses of others.

A stock market helps you do this. It allows you to share in the fortunes of companies like Microsoft, ICI, Cisco, and the risks they take with their (and your) money.

The term 'stocks' is often loosely used to mean shares just as the terms equities or securities are also used for shares. Companies issue both shares and stocks to raise capital. When anybody buys stock, they make a loan to the company that issues it. The coupon or interest rate affixed to the stock gives an idea of the yearly dividend that will be paid for the loan.

Buying shares makes you part owner of the company. You are not a creditor but a shareholder with equity, you have a stake in the fortunes of the company. To take a simple example, the purchase of one share costing £1 in a company worth £100, means you own 1/100 or 0.01% of it.

Example: A shareholding

A merchant has five ships ready to pick up valuable cargo. Four friends put up part of the money for the journey. If the enterprise is successful, they want an equal share of the rewards. If it is not, they lose part, possibly all of their money. In this enterprise, they are shareholders in the same way as owners of shares in the stock market.

One ship sinks. The others return safely with the cargo. Merchant and friends share the profits of the venture, the five of them each getting one-fifth (20%). The total sum they receive is less than it would have been had one ship not sunk, but it is certainly more than they could get by holding on to their money and doing nothing with it. They would lose money, however, if all the ships sank en route, if the cargo could not be sold or the price obtained did not cover the cost of the venture.

So it is with shares. Their prices are not guaranteed to go up. If you sell when prices fall, you could lose some of your capital.

This situation contrasts with bank or other savings where the only loss the capital suffers in those accounts is if the inflation rate is higher than the interest. The value of the capital deposited then falls: a common scenario. Bank and building society failures are such a rarity in the UK they are hardly worth mentioning.

A further bulwark for those institutions and better safeguards for depositors came into effect in December 2001 with the Financial Services Compensation Scheme (FSCS). It replaced eight other arrangements which provided compensation if a firm collapsed owing money to investors, depositors or policy holders. The aim of the new scheme is to provide a cohesive, integrated and reasonable level of compensation for consumers and small businesses who lose money through the collapse of a bank, building society, insurer or investment firm. Deposits up to £33,000 are covered by 100% of £2000 and 90% of £33,000 making a total of £31,700 compensation on the original deposit.

Investments up to £48,000 get compensation of 100% of £30,000 and 90% of the next £20,000, together with long-term insurance at least 90% of the value of the policy holder's guaranteed fund at the date of default.

Risk

There is no compensation for losses on shares. They are risk investments with no guarantee of a profit or that you will get your money back. The trend over the long term has always been upwards – but during that period share prices rise and fall. Before investing any cash, therefore, assume the worst – that you will lose it all. Like summer rain in Spain, this hardly ever happens. When a firm collapses, there is invariably something left in the kitty. But could you bear the loss? If not, don't chance your arm. Play for safety perhaps with Government Bonds (see Chapter 5), or Government sponsored saving schemes.

Attitude to risk

President Truman once quipped, "If you don't like the heat, get out of the kitchen." The same philosophy applies to share dealing. If you can't stand the trauma of seeing your shares slip inexorably downwards into never-never land. then put your money into a building society, bank or other niche where the value of your capital is eaten away by inflation over the years, but just looks as if it isn't. Investment risk can always be minimised and profit enhanced by good judgement, timing and knowledge.

In whatever way you choose to save or invest, and however blue the sky when you start, there is always the chance of a hazard hovering in the heavens. Your capital might seem guaranteed in a bank or similar institution or invested in Government bonds. Changes in interest or inflation rates could alter its value.

Over the last 60 years, the difference in the high and low prices of the Standard and Poor (S&P) 500 index has averaged over 20%, so there is certainly scope for profit there.

According to David Schwartz, a stock market historian, long-term upward trends of around 15 years have often been followed by share prices falling precipitously. A dramatic downturn like this occurred in the late 1980s, yet strong 15-year runs were later enjoyed during 1982–97, 1983–98 and 1984–99. Going back, history appears to repeat itself, see below.

Biggest 15-year percentage rallies followed by falls			
Period	RISE : %	Period	Fall: %
1954–68	165	1959–83	–47
1957–71	108	1972–83	–9
1958–72	146	1973–87	–13

Investors need to be aware of these hiccups and take their profits before the downturns become too steep. If it is any consolation, they will almost never lose all their capital however bad their initial choice of shares may be. Before investing any money at all, however, analyse three things personal to yourself: your attitude to risk; your investment aim(s); and the time period in which you want to achieve the aim(s).

Personal risk

Apart from the basic risks inherent in all financial undertakings, there is your own personal attitude. Financial risk is different from mountain climbing or exploring the jungle, or similar adventurous pursuits in which you may be fearless.

A serious investor must first ask some personal questions. Do you place the safety of your capital before all other considerations? What concerns you most:

(a) its preservation,

(b) appreciation, or

(c) liquidity (that is the ability to get all your money back as soon as you want it; if not immediately, then within the hour, or at least the same day)?

A few general answers can be given here.

If (a), and you are an older investor, short-dated UK or US Government stocks which repay your capital in a few years may be a useful short-term solution, or a bond with a fixed interest and short fixed term, such as those issued by insurance companies. Sound shares with a good history of dividend payouts also suit the older or risk-averse investor.

Another alternative, good for the self-employed in the UK, is a Self-invested Personal Pension (SIIP) where investors put into their own personal pension fund shares which they have bought.

If (b), go for 'blue chips', that is companies with high capitalisation and a long record of growth.

If (c), look around for those banks and building societies which give immediate access to your money and pay the best interest rate on it.

Time span

The amount of time you need to achieve your aims makes a difference to the type of investment or saving best suited to you. In the mordant fashion of children, one of my sons told me that everybody is born with a death sentence on their heads. Only a few people ever seriously contemplate such an event. They may be terminally ill, have seen a terrorist attack and its awful aftermath, live on Death Row or in undeveloped areas of the world where mere survival is a daily struggle. Yet no matter where or how you live, the inevitable visit of the Grim Reaper cannot be delayed for ever. One day there comes an 'appointment in Samarra'.

Until then life goes on, so tailor investment aims against the amount of time normally available to get them. Your age makes a difference to your wants. Younger investors usually seek capital growth. Older ones, a guaranteed income or a lump sum at a particular time to cover a particular lifetime event. Studies of stock markets show that investment in shares in the recent past has proved most profitable over the long term. See Table 2.2 for the performance of £1000 invested in the stock market over 10 years to January 2001.

Retail Price Index	£1325
Building Society Higher Rate Account	£1411
FTSE All-share Index	£3936

Source: Standard & Poor's Micropal: cited Barclays Fund Ltd.

Early saving gives the best returns as the following example shows.

Example: Returns on savings

John and Jan are both aged 30. Jan decides to save £1000 a year for the next 10 years. She stops and John begins at the age of 40. He continues saving for the next 20 years. Their savings earn 6%. This is a high annual return from a savings account, but a useful figure to emphasise the gain made in any form of savings by starting early.

Comparison of early/later saving		
Age	Jan: $	John: $
30	1,000	
31 *interest accrues* ...	1,060	
40 *Jan stops saving*	13,972	1,000
41 *interest continues to accrue* ...	14,810	1,060
50 ...	25,021	13,972
60	44,809	38,993
Gain made by Jan in starting early	**5,816**	

It can be seen that although Jan saved for only 10 years at the rate of $1000 a year, while John saved the same annual amount for 20 years, when they are both aged 60, Jan's savings are nearly $6000 more than John's. The lesson here is save younger, save less, get more.

Reasons for investing

As well as aims, the reasons for investing are also important. You may have some spare cash and want to do something more interesting with it than sticking it into a deposit account. Why not? Creating wealth can be as interesting and stimulating as making two blades of grass grow in the desert sands.

In Graham Greene's novel, *The Captain and the Enemy*, Quigly makes some interesting comments on this point. "Finance comes into everything. Politics, war, marriage, crime, adultery. Everything that exists in the world has something to do with money. Even religion. The priest has to buy his bread and wine and the criminal to buy his gun or his plane."

If you're not concerned about loss, and are not into horse racing, spread betting, poker or similar pursuits, a penny share might be the place for some spare cash. Pick out a cheap share, preferably with a bit of good history behind it, and have a punt on that.

For more specific needs ask yourself whether you want (a) a lump sum at a specific future date, or (b) a stream of income now, or in the future, to supplement a pension and/or make life more comfortable and secure.

Having analysed your attitude to risk, your time span, the amount you have available and investment aims, then decide on the best holdings to suit you. In general terms, the answers to the above questions could be as follows:

Lump sum at a specific date

Getting a lump sum at a certain time means looking for growth with security. The two are not always compatible. Higher risk can lead to greater growth. Risk-averse investors should save regularly each month the same amount in a unit trust or tracker fund, whether it goes up or down. This pound cost averaging uses the rises and falls in the share price to obtain the best value for money over a period of time. It also encourages regular saving.

If you choose a tracker fund you will get nearly the same results over the investment period as whatever index you or your fund manager are tracking, For slightly higher risk, look at split investment trusts and choose a zero preference share maturing at the appropriate date.

You might prefer gilt-edged stock, (or US Treasuries) under par value with the required maturity date. Both are rock-solid safe and comparatively cheap to buy. You will always get the par value back at the appropriate time, although the annual income provided by the yield may be only just enough to beat the inflation rate. An index-linked gilt will protect you against inflation but you cannot guarantee the price of your sell-by date. (See chapter 5 for details on gilts and yields.)

Investing for income

Depending on the amount you have available and the current interest rate, one way of securing an income stream is high yielding stocks or shares. These can be found, for example, in irredeemable stock issued by well-rated companies such as banks. Although such stock is likely to have no growth whatsoever, providing the issuing company is solid you will get a lifetime's income that is likely to be higher than most other conservative investments.

Undated gilts serve the same purpose but, when issued by the UK Government, have a built-in safety factor and so pay lower annual dividends. An older investor might take out an annuity but that means relinquishing capital for income.

The sum available for investment must obviously influence investment choice. For an amount of say £1000 to £5000, choose one or two 'blue chips', sound shares chosen from the FTSE 100 and hold on to them until your chosen date or profit target is reached. If a recession appears likely and you have made a profit on the shares, although not reached your target, compromise and sell half. You can always buy back if the price plummets, and having made a profit, view the shares you are left with as a free gift.

For lump sums above £5000 look at the best performing sectors and choose three or four of the best in those sectors, or go down the FTSE 350 group and pick from them a selection of high yielding stocks. In that group there should be around seven per cent of the stocks listed which offer a reasonable income with the possibility of growth.

Don't get emotionally attached to your shares. In the years 1986–89 growth stocks were considered the 'in thing', yet value stocks, that is 'blue chips', gave 10% better performance than growth stocks. In the next two to three years, there was a turnround.

Although 1990 began well, 1991 proved disastrous for value stocks which underperformed against the market by 10%. They fared little better in 1992, yet a year later, it was the turn of growth stocks to underperform. Their 'growth' did not improve for three years and during 1996–7 value stocks were not much better.

Value stocks tend to perform best over the longer term, but can suffer prolonged bad spells so instead of slavishly following the latest investment fashion, work out your own salvation. The odds against a professional fund manager regularly outperforming the market are estimated to be about four to one. With a bit of knowledge, you can surely beat those odds.

A personal portfolio

The best portfolio should allow for some liquidity. A June 2001 survey by *The Wall Street Journal* of portfolio strategists at sixteen top brokerage firms, showed that on average, they recommended a portfolio blend of assets to include 23.5% in bonds, 69.4% in stocks and 5% cash.

Individual firm allocations ranged from as much as 35% in bonds and 90% stock. Those figures seem too high a ratio of bonds except in a bear market and too high a ratio for stock except in a bull market. One thing is certainly clear. For safety, all your available cash should not be 100% in shares. This may sound like heresy to big investors like Soros, Gann and the Sage of Omaha, Warren Buffett, but that trio is never going to be short of a buck or two.

Have a shot at creating a theoretical portfolio based on your own needs. Watch how your theoretical stocks perform and why and when their prices change. Some stockbrokers allow you to try out a theoretical portfolio before you trade. In this case you need a PC to access their Web sites. For some you will have to register and open an account. This is not the ideal solution when you want a trial run.

The best Web sites are simple and informative. They update share prices and profit and losses and give enough company and investment data for the user to set up a trial portfolio.

Try before you buy

Try one of the many good financial sites on the Internet for a panoply of information on matters referring to money, mortgages and other aspects of personal finance. Many have a deserved reputation for easy access and up-to-the-minute financial information, and allow you to run a 'fantasy' portfolio on their site. Trial runs like these give an insight into the market without costing anything except time. It is akin to looking before you buy. Chapter 4 gives more details on what the stock market offers but some general types of shares can be briefly mentioned here to see how they might fit into a particular portfolio.

Ordinary shares

Ordinary shares in the various stock markets are divided into groups according to the size of their issued capital. The most well-known in the UK comprise the 100 shares, listed in the FTSE (Financial Times Stock Exchange) 100 index, and often referred to as 'blue chips'.There is no reason why they should perform any better than other shares, say in another group like the FTSE 350, except that the 100 which are included in the 350 have more capital. If that amount of capital falls, the offending share is moved downwards into the next level.

Other shares

Preference shares are not really shares at all but loans and holding them makes you a creditor of the company that issues them. **Cumulative preference shares** rate highly in the pecking order, getting the first payout, including previously unpaid dividends. **Debentures** are secured on the firm's assets and are the most secure of all, but if a company goes 'belly up', there may be nothing for anyone.

Convertible preference shares allow holders under certain conditions to convert into shares of the company. In this regard they have some similarities with warrants which entitle the holder to buy the company's share at a fixed price and usually within a fixed time period. **Warrants** can be traded in their own right in the market. **Zero preference shares (zeros)** are often bought for growth of capital and its repayment at a certain fixed date in the future.

From the above list, here are some suggested portfolios, note not recommendations, for different types of investors...

Example: Suggested portfolio for X - man aged 45; aversion to risk; aiming for income and growth

Assuming X has made adequate pension provision, he should choose, according to the amount of cash available, some shares from the FTSE 100 for capital growth. Turn to the next 250 (FTSE 350) and for income, pick out the shares giving the best yield, realising that, generally speaking, the higher the yield, the riskier the investment.

Look also at some of the shorter-term growth bonds issued by insurance companies, or if investor X prefers to leave the management of his money to a fund manager, he might try a unit trust.

He should consider, but not for too long, his tax position and keep some liquid money for emergency or holiday spending in a deposit account giving the highest interest with immediate access. The two are rarely found together. Compromise.

Example: Suggested portfolio for investor Y - student aged 22; likes taking risks; aiming to reduce loan, save for a flat, and one year's travel.

Y has time on his side and should use it. The mnemonics for Investor Y are MM/SL (make more/spend less: easier said than done!) If working part-time he must make sure that he gets at least the minimum wage and save a regular percentage of it, no matter how small.

Although he likes taking risks, there is little risk he can take when his debts are probably greater than his capital and the odds against winning anything on a lottery ticket, for example, make this a futile exercise when income is so tight. He has better odds with competitions open only to students. These are usually costless, get fairly few entries and give more chances of winning something.

Use local or university library facilities to find agencies and companies that fund career development, offer sponsorship schemes or make awards/grants available for studying abroad. One year's world travel as a charity volunteer or in jobs giving board and pin money will not leave Y destitute when he returns home.

He should avoid credit and debit cards as much as possible but if he has to use one, he should pay off more than the monthly minimum or he will be plagued by debt for years. When he acquires some cash – first job? – he wants to put it where he is unlikely to touch it for at least a few years.

Try a short-dated UK government bond (gilt) under par value (a list is available in Post Offices) , or other type of fixed interest with a return higher than a bank's or building society's. When he can pay more off his student loan, he might like to latch on to a cheap share in the stock market and hope it will prove a winner.

Example: Suggested portfolio for investor Z - employed single woman aged 40; aiming to retire early, possibly in five to ten years. She currently holds unit trusts worth around £3000, no shares, and owns her own home.

Retiring early means Z must make bigger contributions to her pension scheme which normally starts paying out at 65 years. That is her first consideration. If her home is in an expensive area and its worth has risen considerably since she bought it, she might consider a future 'swap' for a cheaper one in another area. This will release a largish amount of capital and bigger choices of lifestyle.

For her first direct foray into shares she could look around the stores and shops which she uses. If impressed by the management and products of one, she might consider buying shares in it (so long as it is stock market listed)

Ignoring the ups and downs of the stock market she could also consider making extra regular payments into her unit trust if it is performing well. (See pound cost averaging, above). The regular payments will mount up and should result in a worthwhile portfolio by the time Z retires.

More information on creating suitable investment portfolios for different situations can be found throughout this book, but a few basic investment principles will not at this moment, come amiss.

Basic investment principles

- Keep an emergency fund.
- Attend seminars, read books and the financial press, listen to relevant radio and television programmes.
- Analyse your attitude to risk, your investment aims and the time span needed to achieve them.
- Invest in a speculative share or two, only if you can afford a loss.
- Investments may show no gain for two years or more; unless you have faith in your choice or can afford to wait for a turnround, cut any losses early.
- If you are not using an Internet broker or financial adviser, avoid investing in too many companies because of the monitoring and paper work required.
- As a general rule diversify: that is spread your money in different kind of shares (for example fixed interest stocks, overseas markets and UK companies with a long record of growth). Diversification reduces risks and increases profits. If one share in your portfolio doesn't do well, others may.
- An opposite approach used by some sophisticated investors is focussed investing. Buy a few good shares, hold them and watch them like a hawk; be ready to sell when they peak and buy back when they fall.
- Even if you are a long-term investor, don't be afraid to take a profit.
- For safety, use pound/dollar cost averaging. This strategy involves investing the same amount of money regularly (monthly or quarterly), whether the share price goes up or down. The Table below shows how it works. Check brokers' or fund managers'

charges and use the cheapest unless the dear ones are showing the best returns.

Pound or dollar cost averaging		
Monthly or quarterly investment	**Share price: £/$**	**Number of shares bought**
200	10	20
200	8	25
200	5	40
200	8	25
200	10	20
Total amount invested: 1000	Average price per share 41/5 = 8.2	Total shares bought: 130

Summary

Before creating a personal portfolio of shares, check your attitude to risk, investment aims, the time needed to achieve them and keep to a few basic principles.

Chapter 3

Getting information

*"When it comes to forecasting, there are only two types of economists,
those who don't know, and those who don't know that they don't know."*
Ray Marshall, US Secretary of Labor, 1977–81

Finding out

TO GET the best out of the share market, separate rumour from fact, data
from opinion. Seek out figures, charts and information. Sources are
almost too numerous and you will be faced with an embarrassment of
riches at least until you buy. Some research sources are free, some you
have to pay for. They include the companies themselves, stockbrokers,
the media, the Government, seminars, conferences, books, financial
advisers and the Internet.

The companies

Companies provide a great deal of information about themselves in their
annual reports, but it is not only from the reports that you learn about a
company's management, profit figures, assets, creditors and debtors.
Information about some of these facts can also be found in the company
house magazines and in media sources.

Stockbrokers

It may seem surprising that brokers give out freely such an array of
figures, facts and charts, but they are in the business of buying and
selling shares. To provide information about them informs current
customers and possible future ones. You do not have to be a client of an

individual broker or financial institution. Most are accessible on the Net. They offer graphs of shares over various periods so that you can see the past performance of those in which you are interested, as well as other information which might be of particular interest to you.

Media sources

The media include newspapers, magazines, books, radio and television. Start with the newspapers. Look in the financial pages. They are full of advice and articles on money matters. You will discover, perhaps, that Director A of Company B is leaving shortly. Why? The newspaper will give an opinion. Depending on the prestige of the newspaper and its financial editor, that opinion, whatever it is, will affect the share price.

Check by looking at the current price of Company B's shares in the newspaper. It won't be in what is called 'real time', the price as of now. The page is printed earlier. But there is likely to be a plus or minus sign, probably beside the price, showing the effect of the newspaper's 'revelation' about Director A's move from Company B.

Newspapers

Different newspapers have different ways of listing shares, but all are grouped by sectors, for example, banks, building, engineering, insurance, mining, oil and gas, pharmaceuticals, retailers, technology (the so called dot-com shares which burgeoned in the new millennium), transport, and many others. In some newspapers, Government bonds are also listed.

They show the highest and lowest prices for the year, and sometimes the yield (which is the percentage return on the price of the share). Some newspapers also quote the current middle price of shares which lies midway between the spread of buying and selling prices.

Here's an example of what you may see...

BANKS – up 2.39%						
High (52 weeks)	Low (52 weeks)	Name	Price	+/–	Yield	P/E
862	5231 1/2	Bank of Scotland	793	+17	1.9	17.3
735 ¾	401 1/2	Bank of Ireland	699 3/4	+21	2.5	15.5
2330	1469	Barclays	2101	+61	2.8	12.9
1092	777	HSBC	805	+28	3.7	17.3
772	578	Lloyds TSB	877	+8	4.5	13.6
1785	1005	Royal Bank of Scotland	1540	+19	b1.6	21.0
Souce: *The Daily Telegraph*, London, Friday 13 July 2001						

The first two columns show the highest and lowest prices for the past 52 weeks. The current price, which may have already altered by the time you see it in the press, is the midway price between the price to buy and the price to sell. The spread between the two prices varies.

It is small for frequently traded shares and those in the FTSE 100, commonly known as 'blue chips'. They are the shares of companies with a big capitalisation, where the sum total of shares are of a high value. You can calculate this figure by multiplying the current share price by the number of shares (but the newspapers do it for you).The spread is large for infrequently traded shares, those with a small capitalisation or which are held in a few hands.

Next to the current price you can see how much the share went up or down. In the example shown in the table, the prices were all up.

Yield, in the next column, shows the percentage return on the price of the share. The highest is 4.5% on Lloyds, with the other five yielding 2.5%.

Investors can see that if they are after income, they are unlikely to get it from bank shares on the trend shown over the 52 weeks. Sometimes figures may have a footnote marked by an asterisk or letters of the alphabet. The small 'b' adjoining the Royal Bank of Scotland's yield means 'interim, since raised' that is since the interim dividend on the shares will be higher, the annual return on capital will also be higher than the one that is printed. Even with this addition, the return on capital is still lower, as with the rest of the bank shares, than the best building society rates.

Profit, or gain on capital, is a totally different matter. Gains between lowest and highest points equalled nearly £9 a share (Barclays) over the period shown, down to a quite respectable £2 a share at Lloyds. Investors seeking income need merely slice off some of their capital gain to take the income required. Such 'rewards' are not possible with savings. They show not merely the desirability of investing in shares but the necessity of investing in the right ones at the right time.

The last column gives the P/E, the price/earnings ratio. More is discussed on this topic in later chapters, but, for now, this figure shows roughly the estimated number of years before the shares earn their current price: massively high, although not as high as some of the aptly named, from this point of view at least, 'high tech' shares.

To get an idea of how your bank, building society, unit trust, investment trust, or share purchase is performing, check on the sector average for each of them. If yours are doing better, do not change them. If they are doing worse, think whether your money might find a more attractive home in a different sector.

Magazines

For company news in greater depth, try the financial magazines for:
- profiles of executives in the industry
- company results
- analyses of news and companies' annual reports
- surveys of various international markets
- beginners guides
- takeovers, mergers and new issues.

Also given are constantly updated lists of the best performers in many sectors of the stock market, over short and long periods and much else. Analyses indicate whether it might be the right time to buy or sell stocks in a particular sector, such as banking, pharmaceuticals or mining.

For lighter reading in the magazines, there are reviews of books on personal finance (similar to this one), buy and sell recommendations (some good, some truly bad), and articles by reputable industry figures.

Advertisements

Do not ignore the advertisements. They list many items not so readily available in the news section, for example the commission prices charged by stockbrokers for buying and selling various amounts of shares. This information may help you pick out the most suitable broker for your own eventual purchases and sales.

A note of caution is needed here. When the stock market is making new 'highs', a plethora of advertisements for unit trusts and similar products appear. Do not be sucked into buying them near their top. Note also that when the market is down, the adverts grow less or disappear. This is a good time to consider buying.

Conferences and seminars

The advertisements also tell you about conferences and seminars taking place on aspects of the stock market. At conferences everybody joins in.

It is a big meeting of people 'conferring' on related themes. Seminars are more akin to lectures with guest speakers giving their expertise to the audience. The best are very enlightening and stimulating, with information usually of a very high quality.

When organised by financial institutions, the venue itself is usually at a central location, such as a hotel or specialised conference centre in a big city centre. When organised by other groups or individuals, the seminar is more often held, for reasons of cost, in cheaper venues. All are easily accessible, providing an excellent opportunity to mix with other investors and exchange points of view with them.

A particular attraction of such seminars is that they are attended by an unusual group of participants: the very rich aspiring, like unluckier attendees, to be richer. A very high ethnic mix is usually present, people with different cultures and from different backgrounds. Such an unusual concatenation adds greatly to the interest of the meeting.

Some of the seminars are set up by the executives of firms anxious to sell computer programs which they may have developed. The speakers are, not unnaturally, eagerly enthusiastic to tell you all about their wonderful product. Ignore the *spiel*; concentrate on the information. Much can be learned by those who have no intention of buying anything.

It is the presentation which matters and if made by professionals you can bet your bottom dollar that it will be efficient, well-timed with not a minute wasted and punctual. No mumbling, hesitant speakers but first-class knowledgeable lecturers, and excellent slides illustrate the points made. You cannot fail to pick up something of use, or meet among the audience an expert on some aspect of investment.

Newsletters

Newsletters are a form of communication biased in one direction to suit the reader, for example chartists who buy and sell according to what the charts foretell, traders (who buy and sell frequently often many times in a day,), penny shares for the man or woman who dreams and sees visions, and investors interested in a particular sector such as banking or mining. You have to pay a subscription to receive these newsletters, but many readers feel they are worth the money. Ask for a free specimen copy and judge the contents by their results.

Radio and television

Radio and television add an extra dimension to information on shares. Good programmes come from both. Radio has the advantage of being quick, clearly audible, and able to give company and other financial news almost as soon as it is out. Such news is not limited to the UK, but includes Europe and the USA.

TV programmes, such as *Bloomberg*, blow a breath of vitality into dead as a doornail facts. Various global indices, like the FTSE, the Dow and the Nikkei, are given with their changing figures continuously throughout the day and most of the night, to allow for the different time zones in Europe and America, and there are lively interviews featured with company directors, and fund managers. Competitions and news from investment clubs with their popular appeal also help to enlighten and inform viewers on what appear to be the vagaries and mysteries of the stock market.

Invited guests may give recommendations to 'buy'. Some of the 'tips' are good, and some, at least in the short term, downright awful. Any advice to 'sell' comes sparingly, euphemistically disguised as 'hold'. The advice to sell a particular share or shares will obviously not meet with approval from the directors of those companies whose shares get the thumbs down.

Short answers may be given to phone queries: these nearly always come from men, although women are surely interested in money matters, perhaps more so, but on a lesser scale? For an answer to this conundrum see Chapter 11 on successful systems.

Government sources

Use government and public libraries for finding out about facts like these, which affect individual share prices and the stock market in general. The National Statistics Office sends out nuggets like household spending, the number of people using the Internet, and export and import figures. These may seem to have little bearing on share prices. Investigate further.

If the number of Internet users is static or rising only a little, it suggests that computer and dot-com firms are not likely to see an increase in sales. A rise in the level of imports can indicate too high an exchange rate. Both these increases may lead to a reduction in interest rates and a higher price for Government bonds.

Treaties and agreements between different countries affect current trading patterns as well as specific sectors of the economy. The price of oil, for example, is largely influenced by the Organisation of Petroleum Exporting Countries (OPEC) which aims to coordinate, unify and protect the interest of its members. If OPEC agrees on a price of, say, $21 a barrel, against a current price of $18, oil importers have to pay more. Even if they put up pump prices proportionately, their total revenue is likely to fall. Share prices in the oil sector such as those of BP Amoco or Shell will also fall.

Much depends on what economists call the elasticity of demand for the product, in other words how much will demand be affected by price. If, for example, the demand is inelastic and motorists cannot do without their oil in spite of the price rise, total revenue will be unaffected or may actually go up.

If motorists refuse to pay the new oil price and take to their bicycles instead ('refuse the hike and take to the bike' is a very unlikely scenario), then revenues and share prices will plummet. That you may be a small-time investor is no reason for ignoring political and economic data. John Maynard Keynes found them hugely rewarding. As bursar of King's College, Cambridge, he used the knowledge he culled from studying international currency movements to make a small fortune for the college.

The Internet

Web sites come and go but the best remain to give you information which, when correctly interpreted, can increase your wealth.

Peruse the Internet for good sites. Many cover risk assessment, or fund performance. The Internet can also act as a meeting place for beginners and sophisticates interested in shares. The bulletin boards give them the opportunity to pass on their own tips to others.

However, treat bulletin boards and 'tipsters' with care and a certain scepticism. Investment clubs may sometimes have a lesser fund of knowledge, but as face-to-face sessions they are, in that respect, usually safer than communicating with an unknown 'tipster'.

Analysts on large circulation magazines and newspapers may have a good reputation for their 'recommends', which are often self-fulfilling. A large following take up the tips and the share inevitably moves upwards. A better ruse is to sell on such tips and get yourself out of the exit doors before the stampede.

Other sources

Further advice and information on money matters comes from many different experts, including actuaries, accountants, bank managers, insurance salespeople, and solicitors. Some firms calling themselves financial consultants may be simply insurance and mortgage brokers operating under a new name. In the UK, the Securities and Investments Board (SIB) has a Central Register that details what kind of business a financial adviser is authorised to do.

Financial advisers

A large number of financial 'advisers', including those from most building societies and banks can advise only on the products of the company (and associated companies) to which they are tied. These, of course, may or may not be the best available, or the most appropriate. Their office notepaper and especially their premises must indicate that they are tied to a particular company and are not truely independent advisers. They are usually paid by commission, unlike independents who are paid by fee whether or not you follow their advice.

Independent advisers can choose from the whole market place but, in practice, advise from a range of financial products known to them. Look for magazines and websites which list advisors' particular area of financial expertise, details of their firms and employees, the charges by way of fees and commission in percentage terms and per hour.

Books

Finally, as to the question of investment research from books, here I admit to bias. There is nothing like a book for providing almost timeless information. You do not have to switch on anything; except perhaps the light. There is no need to fiddle with a machine that has a personality disorder and develops a fault just when you need its services most.

In a book you can easily find any item or items you want by looking at the chapter headings or index. There is also usually a glossary to acquaint or refresh yourself with the latest jargon and sometimes a list of references for further information.

It is true that the Internet provides almost inexhaustible sources of material, ideal for research, but news, features, topics are hemmed in by lack of space. There is no room for humour, no space for quotes which enliven the day or encompass, in a few lines, an eternal truth, still relevant even when you're merely trying to get rich.

A book is not so restricted. With luck, there could even be a touch of style or humour in the pages, hard to accomplish on screen with hackers hovering in the wings.

Although newspapers have the advantage of immediacy and the Internet offers the opportunity for encyclopaedic research, for stimulation, enjoyment and enlightenment, there is absolutely nothing like a book.

Financial decisions

After you have collected as much advice and information as is relevant to your circumstances, any financial decisions are still your own. Bear in mind the following points:

- When taking advice from a company or individual make sure that the person or company giving it belongs to a professional organisation.
- If you approach a new financial adviser, be wary about being encouraged to cash in everything and start again. Commission-based salespeople, unlike those who charge fees, are not going to earn anything by telling you to do nothing and keep what you've got.
- Avoid recommendations to switch your money frequently from one fund to another.
- Keep up to date by reading books, the financial sections of newspapers and magazines, and following the money programmes on television and radio.
- On the Internet, treat the bulletin boards as a fun thing, hoping that they might actually produce something worthwhile.
- Keep your emotions in check.
- Avoid the two big hazards that threaten even the richest investors: fear and greed. You will not then be sucked into panic decisions which you will later regret.

Summary

Before undertaking any kind of investment, find out the possibilities of loss and gain through all the research available and listed in this chapter. Take risks only if you enjoy the danger and only with money you can afford to lose. Mistakes once made, cannot easily be rectified.

Chapter 4

What is on offer?

*"The irrationality of a thing is no argument against
its existence; rather a condition of it."*
Friedrich Nietzsche

The stock markets

STOCK MARKETS exist in most big capitals of the world to facilitate
and regulate the buying and selling of stocks. The best known markets
are in Europe, Japan and the USA. One of the world's biggest, the
London Stock Exchange, opens every working day during market hours,
and is regulated by the Securities and Futures Authority. Conditions for
a listing on the main London Stock Exchange are more stringent than
those for smaller or start-up companies and must include a track record.

Other UK markets

Among these 'supplementary markets' are the Alternative Investment
Market (AIM), Ofex and Techmark. None of them has to fulfil the
same conditions for a full stock market quotation as do the companies
listed in the main market. Created in 1995, AIM's object was to raise
capital for new business ventures such as those developing new
processes in the fields of medicine and science, as well as the more
conventional business enterprise.

Although many of the companies have fallen by the wayside, some
have achieved success for themselves and their investors. If you want to
try your luck in this market, take time to find out something about the
product ...and the management. You are unlikely to get any income on
the shares, so you must consider the chances of capital gain. Do not be
diverted by tax concessions such as those recently introduced for
investors in AIM.

Also launched in 1995, Ofex gives private investors the chance to
buy shares in unquoted companies, and the companies the chance to

raise, mainly from private investors, smaller amounts of capital than are usually sought in the main market. Some of the companies eventually go on to AIM and the main market. Others are not so lucky. Neither are their sponsors. Techmark collects companies from a variety of sources which focus on technology, so that they can all be listed in one place and a survey of the sector is thereby made easier for investors. More details of these markets are available from the Stock Exchange, London.

The intermediaries: stockbrokers

Members of the public do not trade directly with the Stock Exchange, but through market makers and stockbrokers, the 'middlemen' between the companies who issue shares and those who deal in them. Market makers are principals who buy and sell shares on their own behalf and trade them in the market. They are gradually being absorbed by big financial institutions for whom stockbroking is one aspect of their business. Brokers get commission on their deals of buying and selling for clients, the private and institutional investors.

You can start investing indirectly by buying a unit trust (mutual fund). Managers and their investment teams choose and buy the shares to go into the fund. The difference between the buying and selling prices of the units is known as the 'spread'. Fund managers then add on management charges and pass these to you, the client.

What is on offer

Investments for purchase and sale in the stock markets trade under a variety of names that can be confusing. As an example, the term 'stocks' normally applied to fixed interest issues, is often loosely used to mean shares. The general term 'securities' covers both stocks and shares while 'equities' is used only in reference to shares.

Companies issue both shares and stocks to raise capital but when you buy shares, you buy a stake in the company. You are part owner, a shareholder with equity in the company. To take a simplified example, if a share costs £1 and the company's capital is £100, you own 1/100 or 0.1% of it. You hope the company will do well and the price will rise; meanwhile you usually get part of the company's yearly profits as a dividend.

Stocks, also issued by companies to raise capital, are loans to a company or, by way of gilt edged stock ('gilts'), to the Government.

Stockholders are therefore creditors of the business, not part owners as are shareholders. If you need ready cash or lose faith in the management, you can sell the stock or the shares. With gilts, management is not so relevant. The Government will stay in office at least until the next election but its policies can influence inflation and other economic trends which affect stock and share prices.

Such a big variety of 'brands' is on offer in the stock market, that there is something to suit every investor: 'ethical' shares for the man or woman who puts morals before money, but prefers to have both; investments which get nothing for a given term and then a packet at a date known when the stock is first bought; shares to give extra income to supplement what is often a miserable pension, and others which combine income with capital growth.

There are also stocks which, ignoring inflation, and barring war and revolutions, are risk free. UK Government stock and US Treasury bonds are examples. Except for the UK index-linked variety, the interest and capital are fixed. Investors know the par value (£100) and unless the stocks are undated (irredeemable) or sold, that par value is returned intact after a given number of years.

Investors also know how much the unchanging annual income will be and when it will arrive. Depending on whether the stock was bought above or below its value of £100, there is either a capital gain or loss over the period to maturity, or when you sell.

Indices

One of the greatest contributions to the theory and practice of investment are the indices. If you regard an index only as an alphabetical list at the back of a book, think again. It is also a measuring device that shows changes of prices or numbers over a period of time and is therefore an essential part of an investor's tool kit. Stock Exchange indices record changes in the prices of different groups of shares. A very early one was constructed by Sir Richard Clark in 1935 when chief leader writer of the *Financial News*.

He, and the editor Mr Maurice Green, having decided to make a regular contribution to financial statistics, planned a modern share index able to reflect the UK equity market's changing moods. In the US there was already the Dow Jones industrial average. When first constituted in

1884 it contained 11 stocks, mostly railways; in 1897 it contained 12 shares and in 2001 it had 30 constituents.

The British 'equivalent' became the *Financial Times* (FT) industrial ordinary share index. Like the Dow Jones, it too was originally made up of 30 shares. Starting with a base of 1000 on the opening date in 1935 they were taken from all parts of the UK economy.

Thirty constituents, all leaders in their fields, was considered the best number that could be chosen: fewer than thirty had less stability, more would iron out any trend and be less sensitive to change. Calculated as a basic unweighted geometric mean (30th root of the 30 shares multiplied by each other), the FT 30 index had the disadvantage that a geometric mean made up from different figures shows a lower result than an arithmetic mean. However, being comparatively small, calculated on an hourly basis, this new index fairly accurately reflected the mood of the market, whereas an index calculated as a basic arithmetic mean would have unduly exaggerated the effect of a change in any one item.

Example: Arithmetic index

Assume there were on 1 January 2002, three large companies; A priced at 100, B at 200, C at 300. You want your arithmetic index to start at a base of 100 to reflect later price changes. So add together ABC giving 600 and divide by six to get 100. Over the next five years, the prices treble to 300 + 600 + 900 = 1800. The index is now 1800/6 = 300 showing the trebling of prices in its constituents. But suppose only A trebles in price. The index would be (300 + 200 + 300)/6 = 133.3, indicating that the index has risen by one third when two of its shares have not risen at all. A geometric mean is not so strongly influenced by individual constituents.

Example: Arithmetic mean and geometric mean

The arithmetic mean of of 2, 2 and 2, (calculated by adding the numbers and dividing by the quantity of numbers = 6/3) is 2, and the geometric mean (cube root of 2 x 2 x 2) is also 2. But with three different figures, 2, 4, 8, the arithmetic mean is 14/3 = 4.67, while the geometric mean is 4 (cube root of 2 x 4 x 8), showing the downward bias of this type of index, which lessens its usefulness for the long term.

The FTSE 100 and others

After the FT 30 came the FT Actuaries All Share index. It encompassed almost 20 times as many constituents. With a weighted arithmetic average, it lacked the distortions of the smaller index and was also more representative of an average portfolio. It was compiled by adding up the market values (or capitalisations) of all companies within the index and then weighting each company by its market value.

Weighting gives a more realistic picture. As an example, the price movement of a larger company that might represent five per cent of the value of the index, has a greater effect on it than a smaller one with a value of say one per cent.

When the new London International Futures and Options Market (LIFFE) opened, however, the All Share Index proved too large for the instant price monitoring necessary for a futures market. The Financial Times Stock Exchange Share Index, popularly known as the Footsie (FTSE) came in as a compromise on the last trading day of 1983.

The Footsie is one of the world's most popular indices with prices recorded minute by minute. It comprises the group of 100 shares with the largest amount of capitalisation. Beginning with a base rate of 1000, the FTSE lacks the distortions of the old FT 30, as it is, like the Standard and Poor's 100 index in the US, a weighted arithmetic index.

More UK indices

Other UK indices are the FTSE 250, comprising the next highly capitalised group of shares, with or without investment companies as you prefer, the FTSE 350 which combines the FTSE 250 with the FTSE 100, the small Alternative Investment market (AIM) and the All Share, giving you a still larger combination with or without the multinational companies.

You can get indices which specialise on high or low yielders and small capitalisations. An index itself is simply a number which represents the market value of all companies in the index at a particular time.

International indices

Indices worldwide include the Dow Jones and Standard & Poor in the US, along with Nasdaq for technology shares. Europe has the Stoxx 50 and Hong Kong has the Hang Seng. The latter has a large number of banks and properties in its make-up and so is used mainly as a short-term indicator. Japan's Nikkei Dow is also somewhat distorted by the high proportion of banks and insurance comapnies. Foreigners have tended to be more interested in high-tech stocks. These can move in quite different directions from the others in the index.

Use of the indices

The main aim of all stock market indices is to reflect accurately the movements in the underlying market. If the whole market moves upwards, few, except some old stubborn laggards, are likely to fall back. Similarly a downward market trend brings down the price of shares and the funds which hold them. By comparing portfolio performance with the appropriate index, the FTSE 100 for example, the ordinary investor gets a more realistic assessment.

Indices also help fund managers who want to create tracker funds or duplicate as far as possible the weighting and constituents of a certain index, usually the FTSE 100.

Calculation

To get the daily index value, the total market value of all constituent companies is divided by an arbitrary number called the divisor. To fix its starting value the divisor is chosen at the starting point of the index and adjusted when amendments are made to its constituents. The value of the index thus remains comparable over time.

Investors need not be overly impressed with funds or managers that 'outperform' the market (more than 70% never do). By choosing and monitoring with knowledge and care your own investment portfolio, you should do much better.

Do not be led astray either by the fact that your own investments or fund have beaten the FTSE by 10%. If it has fallen by say 20%, your own management, like that of many others, has certainly outperformed the market, but you have still made a loss of 10%. The only outperformance you want is a profit.

Sectors

Shares are listed in the financial section of newspapers in sectors. Newspapers vary in the names they use for these categories, but some, such as banks, will be the same in all lists. Sometimes the FTSE 100 are categorised separately for the convenience of readers who only want to deal in the biggest companies by size. On Internet sites, companies have initials by which they are known as well as their company names.

The Financial Times list of sectors includes Aerospace and Defence, Automobiles, Banks, Construction and Building Materials, General Retailers, Health, Household Goods Textiles, Insurance, Internet, Internet e-Commerce, Leisure, Entertainment and Hotels, Media and Photography, Oil and Gas, Pharmaceuticals, Speciality Finance, Support Services, Telecommunication Services, Tobacco, and Transport.

Ordinary shares

Ordinary shares are those which fulfil the very stringent conditions for a listing on the London Stock Exchange. Of these the best known are the 'blue chips'. This US phrase is culled from gambling where the highest value chips were coloured blue. UK 'blue chips' are the 100 biggest companies by size which comprise the FTSE index. They are traded heavily and their prices are rarely ever static.

It is possible to make a profit whether holding them for the short or long term, so they are often recommended as safe bets for pensioners and new investors. Profit is never guaranteed however, and in spite of their high capitalisation, they are not immune from disaster and some occasionally go bust. The FTSE 100 is often listed separately but some newspapers list the FTSE in sectors to reflect the company's main activity in a separate column. Ordinary shares in the main stock market may be regarded, in various ways not always accurately, as 'growth' shares which grow larger and provide good returns for those who hold the shares long term. Income shares are usually recommended because they pay good dividends which provide an income and some (but lesser) capital growth.

'Recovery' shares are those on a downward path but, according to those who recommend them, due for a recovery. They are expected to give good returns to long-term and sometimes even short-term holders and are more likely to be found among the FTSE 350. This includes the FTSE 100 as well as industrials. There are other specific groups which investors may want to check. At the other extreme are the AIM and OFEX markets and the so-called penny shares where you can sometimes make massive profits ...or lose the lot.

Penny shares

Penny shares go under many names, not all polite, but the most common is a cheap share that is one which trades for less than 50p. A stock at that price or less looks cheap and thereby lies its fatal attraction. Let's say you see a penny share at 5p. With only £500, you can buy (ignoring costs) 10,000 shares costing only 5p each. 10,000 shares! You feel rich. They've only got to go up 1p and you've made 10,000 x 1p = £100. If they go up just 5p, you've doubled your money.

So goes the reasoning (if any reasoning goes into the purchase at all) behind penny shares. You get more for your money. It seems incredible, yet it is true and has worked for some lucky investors. But these seductive penny shares have proved a disaster for many more: the companies have gone bust, and the shares melted away like snow in the sun.

It is well to remember when you are hovering in front of a penny share, that the share price itself tells you nothing. What matters is how much each share represents in terms of a company's assets and profits. Another point to bear in mind is the spread, the difference between the buy and sell prices on a share. Long-established so-called 'blue chip' companies are more readily marketable and so have a smaller spread. This makes a difference to your profit when you buy and sell.

Suppose you see the share price of XYZ is 2p. Marvellous! What an opportunity! When you try to buy it, the spread might range from 1.5p to 2.5p. So, you pay a 0.5p 'levy' when you buy, that is a price of 2.5p but get only 1.5p per share when you sell. Assume the share rises to 3p. If the spread has not changed, your selling price will be only 2.5p, which you must exceed to make any profit at all on a purchase. At a price of 3.25p with a spread of 0.5p you get 2.75p per share when you sell. To make that 0.5p profit per share, the price has to rise from the original 2p to 3.25p, that is well over 50%.

Of course if the share price soars into the stratosphere, you will float up with it. Sometimes it does and so do you. The sad truth is, however, that the share is more likely to disappear into a black hole. 'You pays your money and takes your chance'. Buy penny shares only if you enjoy high risks, can afford to lose all your money and can joke not moan about the loss.

Shells

A variant on the penny share is the 'shell', a company whose main asset is its stock market quote. The shell company arranges to buy another company. It then gets control, a ploy known as a 'reverse takeover'. The company taken over now has an easy route to getting a stock market quote. The expanded business looks good and the share price goes up. Shares are issued with a very high rate of interest and were known as junk bonds because they carried a high risk of default. More information on junk bonds is given in Chapter 5.

Preference shares

No matter how named, preference shares are loans to a company and receive fixed interest. The fixed interest of a preference share is just that: fixed. It is paid to the creditors before any dividends go to ordinary shareholders. However, if a company makes higher profits, its share price usually goes up. So usually does the dividend going to shareholders. Fixed interest payments on preference shares remain static. They neither rise nor fall. What does change is the price of the share, and thus its yield, or percentage return on the price.

If, for example, the preference share is issued at par for £100 with an interest payment of five per cent, this 'coupon' of five per cent remains with the share until it matures. That does not mean every buyer always gets five per cent on their investment. If they pay less than £100 for the share, they still get £5. That is more than five per cent of the price and therefore a higher yield. If the share costs more than £100 it still pays £5 a year which is a lower yield than five per cent.

More about the effect of interest rates on yields is discussed in the chapter on bonds. Many investors, however, are more interested in the price they have to pay to get a certain return. When interest rates rise, preference share prices, like those of Government bonds, will fall and vice versa.

Preference shareholders always receive their allotted percentage before ordinary shareholders. How much is left over for these by way of dividend depends on the fixed interest paid to preference shareholders and other prior charges.

If this debt is large, the company is said to be highly geared. In bad times, ordinary shareholders do badly in a highly geared company. In good times, they do well with a bigger payout. The dividend for preference shareholders remains the same.

Example: Simple example of gearing

Company X issues $1m capital divided into 500,000 preference shares of $1 giving 5% interest and 500,000 ordinary shares at $1.

(i) *In an exceptionally good year the profits for distribution are $100,000.*

The 500,000 preference shareholders get 5% on their holdings.

5/100 x (500,000) = $25,000

This leaves $100,000 – $25,000 = $75,000 for the 500,000 ordinary shareholders, that is a dividend of 15%.

(ii) *In a bad year, the profits for distribution are only $30,000. The 500,000 preference shareholders still get $25,000 (5%) on their holdings. This leaves $30,000 – $25,000 = $5000 for the 500,000 ordinary shareholders, a dividend of 1%.*

The company may however decide to 'pass' the dividend and not pay them anything at all. Disenchanted investors are likely to sell their holdings and the share price falls still further.

Convertible preference shares

Cumulative preference shares and debentures were mentioned briefly in Chapter 2. A more interesting type, which brings you into the main market, is a convertible preference share. It allows holders under certain conditions to convert into shares of the company. Although a rise in interest rates pushes down the demand for fixed interest securities, 'convertibles' have a built-in 'extra' over normal loan stocks.

They give the right to convert loan stock into ordinary shares of the company at or within certain future dates. If not converted before the last date, the stock reverts to a normal fixed interest loan stock.

Companies issue convertibles when they need extra capital and bank borrowing is very dear. They replace high-cost secured loans with a lower fixed rate stock. Such an issue works out cheaper than a rights issue which must usually be pitched lower than the share price and may also need a dividend hike to attract buyers.

The advantage to companies of convertibles is fairly obvious. What is the attraction for the buyer? Simply, the convertible offers fixed interest and the option of buying a company share. The conversion rights can be at a premium or a discount to the underlying share. Any rise in the share price brings down the premium and causes the convertible to rise also, though usually much later. One of the advantages of the convertible is its use in a bear market when prices are falling. The fixed interest supports the price.

If you buy a convertible share, when the time comes to convert, ask yourself four questions to guide you in making the decision. Are the company's prospects good? Will there be other chances to convert? When the last conversion date passes and the convertible becomes a straight fixed interest loan stock, will its price fall? If you convert, will the loss of income be acceptable to you?

Convertibles can be bought from brokers like ordinary shares at various commission charges.

Zero preference shares

Zeros are also an interesting variation of a preference share. They are investment trusts, split into capital and income shares. Since the 1960s when they were introduced, they have become more sophisticated with different classes of share. They have a known fixed life and rate of return. When the trust is wound up, there is a predetermined sequence in which the various classes of share are repaid. Zeros come next after the repayment of any loans and debentures.

During the life of the trust the capital shares provide no income. At the maturity date, which, like the redemption value, is known in advance, the assets are distributed, the original capital is repaid, plus any growth arising from the underlying assets of equities, bonds and cash. Being preference shares, zeros offer to holders a prior entitlement to those assets at that date and thus ensure a specific amount of capital at a certain time.

This feature gives the holders some safeguard in falling markets and in periods of high volatility when stock prices move erratically up and down. Appropriate zeros can be selected with the required maturity dates and are tradable on the stock market at any time. In 2001, the longest dated zero was due to mature on 17 March 2017. They offer the chance of low risk capital gains, provision for school or other fees/charges at a future date, or for retirement planning.

Advantages of the income shares are a high and growing income with, in most cases, medium risk. The higher the income desired, however, the greater is the risk to capital.

Cover

Gauging the different levels of risk in individual zeros is achieved by looking at the 'cover'. The trust is 'covered' when asset values are substantially higher than needed to meet the final redemption value. If the underlying assets fall, the redemption value can still be met.

As an example, an eight year trust XYZ, is launched in September 2000. Its price is 100p. Investors are set to receive 190.43p in March 2008. The initial cover is 1.3 times. For every 100p owed to zero holders in March 2008 when the trust is wound up, there is 130p of assets to meet the repayment.

Hurdle rate

Another method of assessing Zeros is the 'hurdle' rate - that is the price which will sustain the predetermined final price of the zero. In the case of the XYZ trust, the initial hurdle rate was 3.49% per annum. The portfolio of the trust could fall by 3.49% per annum and zero holders would still receive around 190.43p per share when the trust is wound up.

Like any other share, zeros can be traded on the stock market. They do not have to be kept until maturity or for any particular period, although, as with equities, the right timing of buying and selling maximises the return.

Irredeemable preference shares

Many investors require income to supplement a pension. Annuities provide these, but are more suited to the older pensioner who does not mind kissing goodbye to his capital as well as his nearest and dearest when the time comes to leave this earthly sod. Younger pensioners may not be so keen on losing their capital when the Grim Reaper calls. Irredeemable preference shares may be the answer to this conundrum.

Issuing companies are obliged to pay the fixed dividend for as long as the company exists. This gives the assurance of a steady income for life with advantageous rates without the holder having to part with capital at death.

The yield is higher than similarly undated gilts to compensate for the lower degree of security but this type of preference share is usually issued by excellent financial institutions with a very high credit rating such as banks and insurers, all graded 'A' or higher by Standard & Poor ratings agency. The issuers are solid, low-risk companies likely to be around for many more years, so irredeemables should prove a safe investment.

They take priority over ordinary shares and are suitable for basic rate UK taxpayers as dividends are paid out of franked (tax-paid) income, so are not subject to basic rate tax.

However, unlike ordinary shares, there is limited growth potential because, as explained above, the capital value of preference shares tends to rise only when interest rates fall. Buy them only if you want a high fixed income, low risk, are not concerned with interest rate changes, and expect little, if any, gain.

With this type of share, as for gilts, timing is important. If you can get in before a fall in interest rates the price of your irredeemable will rise. You will also have a higher fixed income than other comparable investments are yielding. Do not buy them for the short term, or regard them as highly liquid assets. Volatility makes the going tough, and it is difficult to deal in large amounts (you should be so lucky!).

Annuities

Annuities are not shares, but offered by insurance companies who themselves invest in shares. An annuity is thus an indirect investment in shares and could be considered as part of an overall portfolio for older people during a period of high interest rates.

As Jane Austen wrote, 'An annuity is a very serious business', and so it is, for it means relinquishing a lump sum to get income. For people over 70 years old, without heirs, and who come from long-lived families, lifetime annuities may prove attractive.

You put up a lump sum for income payments until you die. The older you are, the higher your income will be. Annuities come in a variety of forms:

- one where payment is guaranteed for five or ten years even if you die within that period
- a joint annuity for husband and wife where the income is paid until the death of the last survivor
- with an escalating rate to (partly) offset inflation
- income for a short fixed term to bridge the gap before an improvement in your circumstances such as redundancy a few years before a pension is due.

Payment is paid in different ways and alters the amount payable. It can be paid in arrears or in advance, half yearly or annually. How much you get on each £1000 of capital depends on the company chosen, the conditions of the annuity and interest rates at the time of purchase.

Disadvantages of an annuity over other investment choices are that unless it is of an escalating type, the annuity income remains fixed from the outset, so you gain most if you buy when interest rates are high. If not, they offer poor value for money. The other big disadvantage, as with any type of pension scheme, is that (unless it is a joint annuity) the pension dies with you and your capital is lost. Where there are no inheritance problems, this might be an advantage, giving you a higher lifetime income.

Levels of risk

No matter how percipient you may be, investing in shares involves five basic risks: company, market, interest rates, inflation rate and exchange rates. Be aware of them. They can be minimised and profit enhanced by judgement and knowledge.

Company risk

Company risk refers to the company in which you might have shares: the profits plunge; the management resigns; banks and other creditors withdraw their loans. The share price drops. So does the expression of the luckless investor. This type of risk can usually be guarded against and, to a certain extent, prevented.

Unless you are a focussed investor like Warren Buffett, keeping a few shares and watching them unceasingly, do not have all your eggs in one basket. Diversify. Watch newspaper reports. Even a rumour of a fall in profits or discrepancy in the accounts can send a share price tumbling. The first loss is the least loss, so get out fast.

Market movement risk

With regard to risk from stock market movements, you are like King Canute who tried to stop the waves coming further up the shore (A false rumour incidentally.) If the American stock market falls, it is more than likely that the European and Asian ones will, too. Different time zones may give you a quick chance to guard against a loss arising from this cause.

Sectors present a different hazard. Falls in one sector can affect the whole market. A drug company, for example, may fail a vital test with its latest drug on which it has spent millions in research and development. The share price falls. As the company is a very large one, it affects the whole sector. The share price of most of the other drug companies will go down too. Depending on the size of their capitalisation, the index will be adversely affected. The stock market moves down in sympathy.

If you have a high regard for the company, stick with them. They will try again or bring out a new product. The share price and the market will recover ...eventually.

Interest, inflation and exchange rate risks

Unless imminent disaster threatens the economy, the monetary authorities responsible for changing the central bank rate (and thereby other interest rates) in their countries, meet at regular intervals. This gives you, the ordinary investor, a chance to gauge what action, if any, will come from those meetings. You will be better able to take the right investment decisions by first checking current government statistics. These might look as stimulating as a page from Money Market Tables (the insomniac's bible) but they help you anticipate these decisions from the top which, like it or not, affect your savings and investments.

As an example, let's say the relevant data shows that consumer spending and borrowing are going up. The authorities want to control the money supply. They increase bank rate to cut down spending and prevent inflation. However, if the balance of payments figures show an increase in imports, the authorities might want to adjust the exchange rate. Will they lower interest rates or is this too simplistic a solution? It is always good to know the score even when you're on the losing side. You get the chance for a few more runs before the stumps are drawn.

The hybrids: unit and investment trusts

In 'hybrids', such as investment trusts, a company invests its capital in other companies and issues shares of its own. This provides a certain amount of safety, for if some shares go down, the others may go up. They may all of course go down together, but that is the risk taken with any share purchase.

Unit trusts, although specific to the UK stock market, have their counterparts in the mutual funds of America. They are neither entirely stocks nor entirely shares although made up of them. The buyer buys 'units' in a trust, formed to buy and manage a pool of shares divided into units.

The units are not usually bought and sold through stockbrokers as is the case with shares, although they may advise such a sale or purchase. The transactions are made through fund managers. More units can be created when demand warrants it, whereas, as a normal rule, companies issue a fixed number of shares. Changes in the demand for those shares directly affect their price; unit trusts will be indirectly affected.

Tracker funds

Over the past few decades some advisers have recommended tracker funds. Normal active fund management involves buying and selling a great number of stocks, in the hope of outperforming the market. Tracking is a passive approach. The fund manager buys, then holds a portfolio of shares which mimics the behaviour of a specific benchmark index such as the FTSE 100 or the Standard & Poor's 500 price index.

Exact replica

To replicate any index exactly, means the fund manager must hold every stock in that index. As this is a daunting and, except for the richest funds, a near impossible task, most tracker funds try for a proportionate likeness. Exposure to large, medium and smaller companies is kept in line with the index being tracked.

Tracker funds do well in good years and are useful for the beginner investor or one with a very low risk tolerance. When the 'copied' index falls, so does the value of the tracker. The investor in an indexed fund can only match the index, never do any better or worse. Around 25% of trackers are estimated to underperform the index.

For home buyers, a long-term tracker fund is sometimes recommended to set up against an interest-only mortgage on the property. In this way only the interest is repaid over the loan period. The outstanding capital remains. It does not decrease as it does with the usual repayment mortgage. The amount saved by paying in this way is put into the tracker fund and kept there for the average 25 years of a mortgage. By this time, it is hoped, the tracker fund will have grown enough to repay the capital outstanding on the mortgage. The idea is that the tracker fund investment will have increased to such an extent that it will also provide enough capital to finance further activities. In theory this sounds an excellent idea. If the property market rises over the life of the mortgage, not an unusual occurrence, this gives the borrower additional security, for it provides an asset value to cover the capital owing on the property.

The safety element is provided by the length of time of the mortgage. However, a word of warning: a tracker fund is not suitable for short-term investment. Neither is it recommended in a period of low inflation as property prices will not increase and may actually fall, while the mortgage rate often remains fixed.

Summary

A variety of shares to suit all investors is available on the world's stock markets. Their indices provide a benchmark against which you can measure the performance of your own investments over time.

Chapter 5

Bonds: price and yields

"An investment in knowledge always pays the best interest."
Benjamin Franklin

Bonds: what they are

ALTHOUGH THIS BOOK is about investing in shares, some investors, particularly older ones and those with low risk thresholds, need the certainty of some fixed interest in their portfolios. In this case, bonds cannot be ignored as an investment choice. They preserve capital and provide income. Finding the right bonds, however, needs care. They are loans, IOUs issued by governments, other state institutions or companies, for the purpose of borrowing money.

When you buy bonds, you become a creditor of the institution to which you have lent your money. No matter whether it is a government, an industrial company, an insurance firm, a corporation or municipality, it promises to pay interest on your capital in the form of a yearly dividend. The validity of that promise depends entirely on the strength and credibility of the institution making it.

If the company goes broke, you will be lucky to receive anything. Capital and dividends go down the drain. If a government goes broke, not only your money but your life may be on the cards. Fortunately in the developed world, this is an unlikely scenario.

As well as government and company (corporate) bonds, there are also bonds from municipalities, for example, state, province or local authority. Their output has almost vanished in the UK but they are still popular in other countries including the USA. Issued by county or state authorities, they are usually only slightly less safe than government bonds. This is why investors get a bigger dividend on them than from corporate bonds, which range from junk bonds to those issued by high quality companies. All have different gradings of security and consequently pay different interest rates.

Government bonds

When interest rates fall, people who rely on income from their savings, lose out.

To compensate for this loss of income, they are sometimes tempted into higher risk investments. A safer ploy is to buy stocks issued by governments. In the USA, they are known as Treasury bonds, Treasuries or T bills, in Germany as bunds. In England they are colloquially referred to as gilt-edged stock or gilts.

Entries used to be made in a gold-edged ledger and this is supposed to be why the stock has the name of gilts. Another explanation is that gilts were thought to be as good as gold, a commodity not altogether the best investment for a portfolio, although against a climate of money laundering, it now has the dubious merit of being internationally acceptable.

When you buy a gilt, you get a certificate stating you have bought a certain amount of stock, its name (for example, Treasury or Exchequer – the names have no significance), the date of repayment (if any), and the gross (pre-tax) rate of interest.

Gilts are categorised by their time before maturity into short, medium, long, irredeemable (undated) or index-linked. Short gilts are redeemed within five years, medium dates repaid in five to 15 years, long dated stocks after 15 years. Index-linked also have a maturity date, but throughout their life move in line with the retail price index.

Irredeemable gilts like Consols or War Loan, are never repaid at all, and are bought for a continuous guaranteed income. Like other gilts, they can be sold at any time. Where there are two dates to a stock, for example, XYZ 10 1/2% 03–06, the Government (or other borrower) can choose to repay at any time between 2003 and 2006.

Some bonds are issued by international institutions, for example, the European Investment Bank (EIB). These have similar security to gilts, but the interest rate (coupon), offered when they are first issued is higher because, for various reasons, gilts are more acceptable to private investors and institutions.

Bond prices and interest rates

The rate of interest that bondholders get depends on the term of the loan and the creditworthiness of the borrower. The economic climate, such as the rate of inflation, the balance of payments and the strength of the pound, also affects the prices of gilts and other stock. Some of these factors can be thought of as the lender's compensation for uncertainty. The longer the term of the loan, the greater the uncertainty of repayment, and therefore the higher the amount that will be demanded for the loan. Inflation, over time, reduces the value of money. A yield curve graphically illustrates the changing yields on a bond with redemption dates stretching into the future. A yield curve shows the relationship between the yield of a government stock and its maturity date. The curve usually slopes upwards because investors hope to gain more from stocks with a long time to run. The longer the term, the higher the yield.

Solvency

Another factor to consider is if the issuer becomes less solvent, unable to pay interest or capital. Creditworthiness is constantly assessed and updated by credit rating agencies such as Moody's or Standard & Poor's. The ratings will doubtless remind some investors of their school or graduate days, the highest grade (with S&P) being AAA, with AA next and lower, going down to the lowest of the investment grades, BBB–, before the non-investment grades beginning at BB+ down to the lowest at B–. Moody's ratings are different with Aaa being top, Aa1 next, and Baa3 being the lowest of the investment grades. Ba1 is the best of the non-investment grades and B3 the worst.

When interest rates fall a close relationship exists between bond prices and interest rates. When interest rates fall, bond prices rise and vice versa. A bondholder of dated or undated stock, can profit from these changes by seizing the opportunity to buy or sell.

Yield

Bonds give a fixed interest return: the lender pays an unchanging payment, often called the 'coupon'. There is a historical reason for this. Bond certificates used to have detachable coupons. These were cashed in when interest payments fell due. Although interest rates are fixed in the prevailing currency, the yield is variable because the price changes.

Example: The effect of interest rate change on bond price and yield

(Note in all the examples which follow, the figures are exaggerated to make the principles clear.)

A government bond, XYZ, costing £100, pays 5% fixed interest. The holder of the bond gets interest of £5 per year, that is, a yield of 5% on the capital sum. Interest rates rise to 10%. The holder of XYZ still gets the same income of £5 a year but a return of £5 on a capital outlay of £100 is only 5%. That is its yield. Who will now buy XYZ at £100 when it pays only 5% on capital? When general interest rates rise to 10% nobody wants stock that yields only 5%.

Demand for XYZ consequently falls. So does the price. It touches £50. At that figure, the annual return on XYZ is still £5 per year, but a return of £5 on capital of £50 is a yield of 10%. That equals the prevailing current interest rate. Until interest rates move from 10% up or down, the price of the bond is likely to hover around the £50 mark.

To calculate the yield or return on a given stock, use the following formula:

$$\frac{\textit{Nominal or par value} \times \textit{Rate of dividend or interest}}{\textit{Purchase price}}$$

Question:

If £100 stock pays 12% fixed interest and costs £120 to buy, what is its yield?

Answer

$$\frac{\textit{(Par value) £100} \times \textit{12 (rate of interest)}}{\textit{(Purchase price) £120}} = 10\%$$

Running Yield (gross)

The nominal yield on a stock is the interest paid, expressed as a percentage of its par value, that is £100 in the example above. The running yield depends on the price of the stock. It is calculated by multiplying the nominal value (£100) of the stock by its interest rate (coupon) and dividing by its market price.

Example: Running yield

Nominal price of Stock:	Coupon: %	Market price of stock:	Received per year:	Yield: %
100	12	100	12	12
100	12	200	12	6
100	12	50	12	24

Calculations:

$$12 \times 100/100 = 12\%$$
$$12 \times 200/100 = 6\%$$
$$12 \times 100/50 = 24\%$$

Gilt strips

A new type of gilt-edged stock was introduced in 1997. Called a 'strip', it breaks down a conventional gilt into two parts, either of which can be traded separately. A ten-year gilt, for example, normally pays dividends twice yearly until maturity. Under the new arrangement it is stripped firstly into 20 interest payments, which pay dividends in six monthly instalments over the length of the bond.

The capital element is sold separately. As all interest has been stripped from it, the bond is usually sold at a discount. The investor thus gets a capital gain at the end of the ten-year period, although like all gilts a strip can be sold at any point during its lifetime.

The object of the strips is to provide income for those who only require this element; while the capital part of the strip, being free of gains tax, suits the needs of some investors, and particularly those financial institutions with large amounts of capital to invest. In essence, the capital 'strips' are similar to zero preference shares, paying nothing out until the maturity date.

Gilt prices

Prices differ for different gilts. So does the interest rate, colloquially known as the 'coupon': Two and a half per cent is a low coupon, 14 per cent, a high coupon. Interest on all UK Government stocks is paid half-yearly, except for Consols, on which it is paid quarterly. Index-linked varieties of gilts add the rate of inflation on to the capital. The return of capital is guaranteed by the issuer when the IOU is redeemed at its face or par value, usually £100. This happens at the maturity or redemption date when, except for undated stocks, the loan period ends.

Nominal or face value of stock and market price

The nominal, or face value, of stock, also known as its par value, is the price when first issued. With gilts it is £100, (or with US Treasuries, $100), the price at which the Government redeems the stock at maturity. For instance, the face value of XYZ 12% 2005, when first issued at par, is £100, and when held until 2005 repays £100 for every £100 of stock bought.

If you buy XYZ during any period of its issue, no matter what the nominal price or face value of the stock, you still get £100 on it at maturity. So if you sell XYZ before that date and, depending on the price you paid, you may gain or lose on the transaction (although you get interest throughout the life of the stock).

The market price of XYZ like all other stock, moves up or down with the demand for it. The actual percentage interest you get on any stock you buy (its running yield) depends on the price you paid for it.

If you hold on to a stock until redemption, and you paid more than £100 for it, then you will make a loss on your capital, even though you may have received high interest throughout the life of the stock.

Redemption yield

The yield to the maturity date, known as the redemption yield, is always quoted gross. The redemption yield includes both the running yield and the gain or loss (termed 'points') of the gilt over the period of time until its par value is redeemed at maturity. It is a figure of greater importance to large holders of gilts (such as financial institutions, pension funds, unit trust managers) than the running yield, because gilt capital gains are tax free, whereas income is taxable.

An approximate calculation is shown below. In practice, redemption yields are calculated using more complicated formulae that take compounding into account.

Example: Gross redemption yield (Gain)

*A 10% stock has a market price in 2002 of £90 and is redeemable in
2012 at £100. What is its gross redemption yield?*
(a) Points to redemption (par value – market price) = 100 – 90 = 10
(b) Years to redemption = 2012 – 2002   *= 10*
(c) Divide (a) by (b), i.e. 10/10   *= 1.00*
(d) Running yield = 10 × 100/90   *= 11.10%*

Adding (c) to (d), i.e. 11.10 + 1.0 gives
Gross Redemption Yield   *= 12.10%*

Example: Gross redemption yield (Loss)

*A 15% stock has a market price in 2002 of £120 and is redeemable in
2012 at £100. What is its gross redemption yield?*
(a) Points to redemption (par value – market price) = 100 – 120 = –20
(b) Years to redemption = 2012 – 2002   *= 10*
(c) Divide (a) by (b), i.e. -20/10   *= -2.00*
(d) Running yield = 15 × 100/120   *= 12.50%*

Adding (c) to (d), i.e. 12.50 – 2.0 gives
Gross Redemption Yield   *= 10.50%*

How to buy and sell

Gilts can be bought direct from brokers, banks or by post from the Bank
of England through the Debt Management Office. The cost of
commission is 0.7% for the first £5,000 with a minimum of £12.50, £35
up to £10,000 and 0.375% for amounts above that.

Although cheaper than most brokers, there is a disadvantage in using
the postal service of the Debt Management Office (Bank of England),
namely the delay in dealing. You do not know the price you will pay for
the stock, as you do when using a broker, although you can put limits on
the amount or value of stock you wish to buy.

Commission charges can change at any time. Check before you buy.
Brokers use their own scale of charges which can change at any time. A
typical example would be a charge of around 1% with a minimum charge
for the first £10,000 of stock, 0.5% for the next £10,000 and 0.25% for
the next £10,000.

Any gilt bought for under its par value of £100, and held until maturity, will provide both an annual dividend sum as well as the nominal return of capital, although, (except for index-linked stock), it may be depleted by inflation.

Junk bonds

Junk bonds carry a very high degree of risk. They are the equivalent of writing out a cheque with only a faint chance of seeing the money return or the product bought. The gamble – junk bonds are nothing more – sometimes comes off. For high rollers and others who like to take big risks, these bonds can provide a bit of adrenalin if nothing else. As investor, Warren Buffett, is reported to have said of a wave of such buying in the States, "Mountains of junk bonds were sold by those who didn't care, to those that didn't think – and there was no shortage of either".

First issued a few decades ago in the USA, these bonds were originally designed to finance the takeover of a large firm by a smaller one. The smaller company borrowed heavily on their own limited assets and those of the target company by issuing bonds. This buyout resulted in the emerging company having a very high ratio of debt to equity.

The bonds issued to finance these acquisitions became known, not unkindly in view of their tendency to go AWOL, as junk bonds. The name has stuck. Junk bonds are still around both in the UK and USA, offering very high interest rates on money lent. If the company can ever turn round and take off, instead of their usual descent into a bottomless pit, they might become every investor's dream of a 'ten bagger', the jargon for initial capital multiplied ten times.

Corporation bonds / irredeemables

Bonds issued by companies may be good or bad risks, depending on the worth of the institution issuing them. A variant of the straightforward bond with a par value and maturity date are irredeemable preference shares. Like irredeemable gilts, they are bought and held for income.

In this regard they are better than an annuity which equally provides a lifetime's income, but the annuity does just that and no more; in other words, when your life ends, so does the annuity. Capital and income are both extinguished. This is not the case with irredeemables. They become part of your estate. If you have no heirs, this may not concern you at all, but the stock can always be bequeathed to a favourite charity.

Irredeemable gilts and shares, like dated stock, have a fixed dividend, with a higher yield than comparable bonds because, (a) they do not have such good marketability, and (b), in the case of shares, their rating depends on the quality of the issuing company. Usually these are solid, low-risk institutions such as banks and insurers, graded A or higher by the credit ratings agency, Standard & Poor's .

The banks take this route to raise this type of capital to cover liabilities obligatory under international banking rules. They and the other issuing companies are hardly likely to fail, so the shares make a good bet for risk-averse investors. However, there can be a wide spread between the buy and sell prices. Furthermore prices can show a surprising volatility with a swing of 20 per cent in six months.

This makes irredeemables tempting for short-term trading except for the wide spread. This must be taken into account. It adds considerably to costs. If you have large amounts of stock, £100,000 or more (you should be so lucky!), much of this could be lost by bad timing.

Gilts are safer, but more has to be given up in terms of yield for this element of safety. Neither irredeemable gilts nor shares are as marketable as the dated kind and they are more vulnerable to the influence of inflation and interest rate changes. They also have little growth potential unless interest rates fall precipitantly after their purchase. Their price could rise in a low inflation/interest rate climate.

Points to consider

When buying gilts or any fixed interest stock, consider:

- the risk...(negligible in the case of gilts, extremely high for junk bonds)
- whether you prefer high yielding stocks or the chance of capital gain, which on gilts is tax free...(but you cannot offset losses against gains elsewhere)
- that dividends are paid gross...(useful for non-taxpayers and overseas buyers)
- that there is no capital gains tax...(but losses cannot be offset against other gains)
- the risk of loss if you have to sell the stock at the wrong time.

High taxpayers might consider low coupon stock bought at a discount. Discounting estimates the value of a money claim at some future date by reference to the current interest rate. It gives the answer to such questions as 'how much should I receive now for giving up a claim to £500 in two years' time if interest is at 15%?' The answer, using a similar formula to that for compound interest, is £378 072. A low coupon stock sacrifices income for capital gain when the stock matures ...useful for high taxpayers.

If a regular flow of income is important, choose six stocks with different monthly interest dates. Interest is paid twice yearly, providing a monthly dividend until the stock is redeemed, when the capital is repaid at par value.

Gilt unit trusts

Gilt unit trusts sometimes give higher returns than gilts bought direct because the management of a gilt portfolio can be difficult and time consuming. Another reason is that whereas fund managers can, in theory, buy all the gilts which make up the FT Short Gilt Index, such a course of action is impossible for the ordinary investor who also has to watch charges on the trust. These can sometimes be dearer than buying gilts direct.

Fund managers of gilt unit trusts often get better prices because they deal in size, can switch more easily and cheaply into bonds of different maturity dates, and buy and sell to take advantage of anomalies in yields and prices. Trading like this exposes them, however, to two dangers. Unlike the private investor, they rarely hold gilts to maturity but buy and sell to boost yield and the fund's income. In so doing they risk some loss of capital. Aiming for capital gains AND income is not so easy as it might seem.

Capital losses may also arise instead of gains when they buy in the expectation of a fall in interest rates and the Bank of England (or Federal Reserve Board) do not oblige. Falling interest rates usually cause a currency to weaken, so movements in and out of sterling denominated bonds need to be carefully monitored. In this regard, trust fund managers have an advantage over the private investor who cannot switch so easily and cheaply from one currency to another.

It is not easy to compare performance figures. Rankings can be found under gilt and fixed interest, and international fixed interest, listings, but funds have different mixes of gilts and bonds, from different countries and institutions.

Dublin based unit trusts distribute income gross, an advantage for the non-taxpayer, or overseas buyer. If you invest in stock overseas, check in what currency the fund is denominated. You could lose out if you sold your units and withdrew your cash in a depreciated currency, whatever it might be.

Summary

Bonds are:
- fixed interest investments,
- of short-, medium-, long-term, and indefinite length,
- issued by governments, other state institutions and companies.

Their:
- price is affected by interest rates,
- yield is the percentage return on their price.

They:
- offer varying degrees of interest and risk, dependent on the coupon and issuing institution,
- can be bought for income or capital gain,
- are repayable at par value on the maturity date of the bond.

Chapter 6

How to buy

"...the best time to buy stocks is when you have money."
Sir John Templeton

Spoilt for choice

HAVING SEEN what's available on the stock markets and the advantage of long-term share holding over deposit accounts, you now want to invest some cash and create a portfolio of your own. You must find a stockbroker who will buy and sell for you, or, in the case of unit trusts, a dealer who will buy the trust and sometimes discount the charges. Three options are then open to you:

● to choose an execution-only service in which case you rely on your own judgement and all the profit or loss will be on your own head,

● have an advisory service in which case you can praise or blame the resulting gain or loss on others (although it won't ease the pain of a loss), or

● to go for a discretionary service where you pass over to someone else the whole job of managing your financial affairs including investments.

Being your own judge ...and jury

If you want to go your own way without advice or help with financial planning and have done sufficient research to go into the market with your eyes open, how do you buy a share in a particular company? You use one of the market retailers, the stockbrokers or a financial institution such as a bank which provides stock broking services.

You may get a recommend from a friend who is already a client giving you the name of a stockbroker specialising in individual investors. Follow this up. Getting the right broker is only slightly less important than creating the right portfolio. Have no qualms about being a 'small' investor; it's your money you are shelling out, not the broker's and you want the best value you can find.

Stockbrokers and market makers

Stockbrokers are a varied bunch with no uniform pricing systems, other than the stamp duty which they must add to the purchase price of a UK share. They may be members of a large financial conglomerate operating in the City interested mainly in institutional business, or an independent company with a private clientele.

They could be one of the diminishing group of market makers, principals dealing with shares they own and so able to determine the price for that share. If this is the case, you should be told.

A free directory of private client stockbrokers and their services is available from the *Association of Private Client Investment Managers and Stockbrokers* (APCIMS). *The Independent Financial Adviser Promotion* (IFAP) similarly produces a directory of their members' addresses, fees, specialisms and services.

High street banks are taking an increasing share of stockbroking services, often provided at the touch of a button. Even if your branch bank does not offer these, it will probably be able to buy and sell shares for you through a stockbroker. The bigger building societies also offer share-dealing services. Other intermediaries like IFAs, although not members of the London Stock Exchange have an advisory service which includes placing your orders with a Stock Exchange member firm. If you trade online (see below) confirm by checking in the UK with the FSA, that the provider of the service is properly regulated.

Some stockbrokers stipulate a minimum size of investment before they take you on, or they may want to establish how active an investor you are likely to be as this sometimes affects the price they charge. Before contacting any broker, do a little research and come up with some ideas of your own. You are then better able to judge the value of any advice. After you have decided the kind of firm you want to deal with, shop around to find the best one to suit your purpose and able to supply the service you want.

Execution only

Being your own decision maker means choosing an execution-only service for dealing. There is no personal advice. You ask to buy or sell a certain share or shares, and the brokers you choose execute the order, nothing more. However, they may send information, mainly through newsletters on individual shares and the stock market in general.

An execution-only service is available (a) by phone or post, through banks, building societies and the specialist telephone services or (b) online using your personal computer accessing the Internet.

The big disadvantage of using the post is the slowness of response. By the time your order has filtered through the mail, the price you hoped to get will probably have long since gone. And if the mail delivers your cheque after the due date, the broker may impose a penalty for late payment. Using the post is best reserved for the buying or selling of gilts.

The phone is slightly quicker but holding on through interminable musical renditions makes you wonder whether you've homed on to a Wagnerian opera and whether tomorrow's snail mail will arrive first. The share price meanwhile goes up and down so fast, that dealing becomes more like a game of poker, suitable for the high roller, not the nervous beginner.

As a phone or postal client you receive both a contract note and later, a share certificate. These record your transaction and prove your ownership of the share. You also get any shareholder perks that may be around, company accounts and invitations to shareholders' meetings where you may vote on issues previously notified to you.

Online dealing

An alternative method of dealing which avoids the use of certificates altogether means using the Internet and therefore a computer. Not everybody has a PC and not everyone who has wants to use it for share dealing. To trade online you will still need brokers' names, as well as their range of services and commission rates. Names and Web sites are listed in the financial columns of newspapers and financial magazines.

Bearing these facts in mind, you choose an online broker and a registration form appears on the computer screen. Complete this, and accept the 'disclaimer' (protection against money laundering), download the page and send it to the chosen broker with your cheque.

You will receive a password, PIN and sometimes a nominee bank account. After that and providing your cheque has been cleared, registration is immediate. You can start dealing. Later by post comes a 'welcome' letter and possibly a cheque book, (not available through all brokers).

When you want to buy or sell, log on to the site by entering your user name and password both of which are given to you when your account is opened. You will see a series of questions such as whether you want to know the current value of your portfolio, or receive share information, or see graphs of particular shares.

Click on 'trade', and quote your 'trading' name, also given to you when you first open an account. Enter the name or code of the share you want to buy/sell, or use the 'search' facility if you do not know the code, and then state a price limit. You may be told that this price is not possible. Two alternative prices will be given to you: 'bid for sales' and 'offer for buying', the difference being the 'spread.'

Decide whether or not you want to deal at this price and click the appropriate button. You will later get through the post a record of the transaction (instead of a share certificate). Keep it carefully in case you ever need to prove ownership of the share.

Disadvantages of online trading

As a new customer, you pay for the first trade by cheque but later deals are charged by direct debit from your bank account. Although rapidly increasing in the US, online dealing still accounts for only a minority of all UK trading. There is no doubt that it is quicker, cheaper and usually more efficient. Whether those advantages are enough to compensate for the drawbacks of the system, is a matter for the individual investor.

You may, for example, find that your UK online broker cannot deal for you when you want a particular number of shares. You will be told that only the Normal Market Size (NMS) is possible. Depending on the cost of buying and selling, this amount will not give you enough profit margin. You will want to phone the broker for an explanation. That could take you longer than you bargained for.

When there is a flood of online requests to sell a particular share the NMS may be reduced from say 1000 to 100. Another factor to contend with is that, although commissions are coming down, an annual fee ranging from £10 upwards may be added on to an account for running it. You are not always aware of this when you sign on.

The fee covers the supplying of charts, company reports and similar items, although it may also include the running of the bank account from which you pay for the shares you buy. Another hitch might be the electronic system used by the brokers. It is not infallible. Just when you are on the verge of a tremendous breakthrough, that is the one time when it will break down. Nothing can be done about this. You just have to take the possibility on board. But you can check fees and whether the broker has a good phone back-up if you need to contact him urgently. Depending on the number of deals you wish to make, it may be worth your while to have a secondary stock market account with an 'offline' broker. This can prove very useful when you are running a bit short of cash, see an excellent buying opportunity, and are awaiting your salary or other payment.

Unless the money for the share purchase is already in your account, you cannot usually buy online (although some brokers will accept credit cards). By the time you get your cash upfront, the share on which you have your eagle eye will have risen too high for you to catch it. If you have a 'phone' broker, the problem is solved. You can buy the share and pay for or even sell it by settlement day, laughing all the way to the bank.

Most UK investors, particularly women, still prefer to deal by phone or post through building societies or banks. They find that buying or selling shares in this way is simple; they get any share perks on offer, and the certificates they receive, prove their ownership of the shares. Investors are also free to choose any brokers they want for any deal, and transfer their shares without any charge being levied.

By contrast, changing a share registered online might cost a substantial sum for each line of stock. Transferring ten or more could make a big dent in any profits. Another advantage of postal or phone trading with calls recorded is that no money has to be paid upfront before dealing begins and, except for the occasional mishap, it is reasonably safe.

With online dealing, investors receive confirmation of their holdings in electronic form, not as a tangible share certificate. The nominee account in which shares usually have to be held, militate against free transfer or sales through another broker, and shareholder perks must usually be foregone. Money has to be paid upfront before any dealing can begin but when you sell a share, you do not have to wait for the cash. It goes immediately into the account opened when you begin online dealing.

Unless a hacker breaks into the system, or you lose/forget your logon password/number, the electronic system is also arguably safer than phone/post trading. The bank account records all dividends, interest and other money paid in or out, This simplifies record keeping and tax calculations. For the richer, older investor, it also helps will-making or other transactions made to reduce tax liabilities.

You can see the current prices of your shares at a glance, how much their prices go up or down, the total value and percentage change of your portfolio since it was started.

Taking advice

For anybody feeling slightly wary about dealing for the first time, the traditional (and dearer) advisory stockbroking service might be better than the execution-only, home-alone type. Contact the person who will deal with your account. Discuss your investment objectives. He will probably want details of your income, commitments, and attitude to risk. These facts help ascertain whether you need investments for income, or growth. They also help the broker to create a portfolio that meets your aims and the level of risk acceptable to you.

Minimum commissions per deal are higher than the execution-only service. This gives access to the firm's own research and investment analysis (which incidentally may be also available free of charge on other sites) as well as a platform for your own ideas.

The broker may offer investment suggestions but, with a non-discretionary advisory service, all decisions about what shares to buy or sell are yours alone. Nothing will be bought or sold without your agreement.

Some advisory services are minimal: merely responses to your requests for advice on specific shares. In the more active (and dearer) kind, the stockbroker also checks your whole portfolio and provides other services, such as regular valuations.

Passing the buck: discretionary service

You may feel happier handing over all your financial decisions to others, including investment. There is no guarantee that professional advisors will do better than anybody else, including yourself, unless they have an excellent track record which, with luck and judgement, will continue. If you are contemplating a not quite so intrepid foray into the stock market, brokers and IFAs offer portfolio management as well as execution-only and advisory services.

Portfolio management could include annual valuations, advice on tax planning, stock market information, administrative paperwork and safe keeping of share certificates. A consolidated annual fee may be charged for these services, or a separate charge for each service required.

You and your broker should both be very clear as to whether the service you want is to be discretionary or non-discretionary. In the former, the normal route for portfolio management, the broker takes decisions for you; in the latter you make your own. By taking the discretionary route of portfolio management, your investment aims are established, and shares bought or sold on your behalf. You will not be consulted about this but informed after each deal.

Cost

Stockbrokers earn their living on the commission paid by clients for whom they buy and sell shares. Rates and costs vary from firm to firm. Some stockbrokers stipulate a certain size portfolio of perhaps a minimum of £100,000 before they will take anybody on their books. Others may try and steer clients with less than, say, £50,000, into unit trusts instead of shares.

But, as the APCIMS directory shows, there are plenty of stockbrokers requiring far less than £50,000–£100,000 as a minimum trading capital. Their commissions may be quite cheap for small deals. The cheaper the minimum charge, the more likely it is that the firm runs a low cost service for small private investors and is happy to have them on their client list. Intermediaries such as IFAs can add their own charge if they deal with a stockbroker on a client's behalf.

As costs are so different, check them carefully. Some brokers make concessions for constant trades, others for small amounts, others for larger amounts. An introductory offer might be made of a very low charge for a month as a kind of loss-leader.

Charges are coming down, but not nearly fast enough. Some brokers offer special rates for frequent trades, cheque books with interest bearing accounts, newsletters, bulletin boards, free research and 'tip sheets'. A fee is often charged for the administration of the account including the banking element.

The money deposited in the bank gets a higher rate of interest than an ordinary deposit account. A cheque book, not always available with other so called 'high' interest rate deposit accounts, maybe also provided.

There is the inevitable stamp duty (minimum charge of £5) paid to the Government. It is added to the cost of any shares or unit trusts that you buy but is not payable when you buy shares in the US or other foreign markets. A contract note is sent out to record the deal when it is completed. Keep it for your own records.

As already noted, a particular advantage of online dealing is the price. Phone trades might cost in commission 1% up to £3500 and 0.1% above, with a set minimum for any one phone trade. Add on 0.5% stamp duty and these charges soon make a dent in a small profit. Even allowing for these 'extras', however, the cost of two lots of commission for buying and selling plus stamp duty on purchases often seems disproportionate for an investor dealing in small amounts.

Forage around for one of the 'cheaper' brokers. Take care. Charges vary and the variation can make a big difference to your dealing costs. Some brokers have a sliding scale depending on the number of trades and the amounts; others a flat rate. It is also difficult to compare online brokers' costs because of their different charging structures: percentage cost, minimum and maximum cost or special offers.

Whether you trade by phone or online, current UK legislation requires that you sign an agreement with the broker before they can trade on your behalf.

Very large savings can be made by using the 'right' broker. As an example, if you make deals in UK stocks of £5000 every week the charges could be as low as £390 or as high as £2600. Such an example is hardly likely to tempt the beginner investor holding a few shares. The saving made by switching to a 'cheaper' broker could well be eaten up by the cost of transferring shares. Here lethargy will surely take over, for banks might have to be changed, too.

Paying for shares

Unlike phone dealing where you pay after your deal, with online transactions it is usual for the 'customer' to have money in an online account before a share can be bought. You will not pay or be paid for stock market transactions immediately.

The account period has altered over the last years. Previously you used to be able to buy and sell shares without paying or being paid for them until settlement day. This arrived ten days after the account period and showed all the deals made in that time, along with the balance payable or receivable. Such a comparatively long wait, very favourable to buyers, has now been abolished in favour of a 'rolling settlement'.

Each transaction must be settled five working days after the dealing date so any day could be a settlement day. There used to be a period known as 'bed and breakfast' by which shares could be sold on one trading day and bought back the next. The object was to avoid the tax on capital gains levied in the UK on sums over a certain amount (this changes yearly – in 2001 it was £7,100). This particular manoeuvre has now been almost wiped out by making a 30-day period between buying and selling shares, but it can still be worthwhile if you have bought stock showing gains much above the point at which the tax begins to bite.

Contracts

The contract note shows the date by which purchases must be paid for and/or the date on which you will receive payment for sales. When several transactions are made on the same day, you get an advice note for the total settlement due, along with the contracts for those sales.

You can make arrangements for late payment, but it is expensive, and you may have to pay 25% of the deal upfront. Some brokers will not deal unless the client has cleared funds. A bank account may be set up online to receive these funds. Interest is paid on them but there is often a small annual management charge. Ask for particulars.

Some stockbrokers accept payment by credit card over the phone or give you ten days to pay following a transaction. Or you may set up an account with the firm so that money is already there to meet the cost of share purchases.

Since the introduction of CREST, a system which registers, transfers and settles stock market transactions electronically, some investors find it more convenient to hold their shares through nominee accounts organised by their broker.

Although you may hold your shares like this, as the 'beneficial' owner, you continue to receive dividends but get no share certificates and your name will not appear on the share register. Neither will you get the company's annual reports, nor invitations to its annual meeting where you have the right to vote.

You might also lose your entitlement to any shareholders' perks offered by the companies, although such perks are becoming more of a rarity.

In spite of these disadvantages, many investors prefer nominee accounts. They may be able to become a sponsored member of CREST so avoiding the paperwork but getting all the rights of registered shareholders such as annual reports, any correspondence of interest, invitations to shareholders' meetings, etc.. If the broker can offer you membership, ask if there are any charges for this option.

Keeping records

When you deal online, take care of the contract note as it constitutes proof of the transaction. With phone or post dealing the share certificate received is proof of ownership. Details of your investment income may be needed for your tax returns. For this purpose and your own information, buy an investor's ledger, or make one from an exercise book. Use one page to record purchases, the facing page for sales and the back page for dividends.

Purchases					
Name of share	Price	Commission	Number of shares	Total cost (commission plus price and stamp duty)	Date of purchase
Sales					
Name of share	Price	Commission	Number of shares	Total received	Date of sale

You need to record dividends for the tax authorities (the only people ever likely to check you are not salting away millions) and for yourself. Alternatively, several software packages such as *Microsoft Excel* make easy recording of incoming and outgoing funds.

Lost certificates

For some reason the contingency of lost share certificates has rarely been mentioned in investment circles until recently. Yet this is not such an uncommon occurrence when dealing with the affairs of a handicapped or deceased relative. Search for records of transactions such as contract notes or dividend vouchers. Cheque stubs and bank accounts may also be available to help you to find missing certificates.

Having found as much information as you can muster, write to the appropriate Registrar, (when you know the company's name, you can soon find the Registrar). Give circumstances of the loss and relevant dates. You may have to swear before a commissioner of oaths (free) that the account you have given of the loss is a true one and you will have to pay for a duplicate certificate.

A new organisation was set up in 2001 to help in the search for lost paper assets. Known as the *Unclaimed Assets Register* (UAR), it enables investors to find unclaimed dividends and windfalls. Supported by many leading financial organisations, and FTSE 100 companies such as AstraZeneca, BP, BT, the Lattice Group, Prudential, Royal & Sun Alliance, Scottish Widows and Vodafone, the UAR already holds data relating to owners of lost or forgotten life policies, pensions and unit trusts.

Its orbit is now extended to incorporate unclaimed dividends and related securities which are believed to amount to over £3 billion.

According to the UAR's manager the main reason for investors losing track of their shareholdings is their own failure to inform registrars of a change of address. With 1.5 million house moves a year and so many pressing things to think about when relocating, share registrars tend not to be top of the list and can often be permanently forgotten.

Moving, marrying and dying are the main causes of a lost investment. Company name changes do not help. Since 1995, 44 of the FTSE 100 have undergone a name change or a takeover. Some people fail to appreciate the importance of documentation whether these be share certificates, life or pension policies.

Lack of care often leads to loss of documentation, with 'boring' paperwork eventually finding its way to the rubbish bin. An estimated £15 billion of financial assets are unclaimed by the public. This breaks down into life policies £1 billion; personal pensions £3 billion; shares and dividends £3 billion; bank and building societies £5 billion; National Savings £3 billion, the Lottery and others £300 million. Over a period of 18 months, the UAR reunited in excess of £1.3 million with its rightful owners with the amounts recovered varying from 92p to £36,000.

The UAR, a global insurance brokerage, with consulting and insurance underwriting subsidiaries, is a wholly owned subsidiary of

Aon whose common stock is listed on the New York, Chicago, Frankfurt
and London Stock Exchanges.

Odd numbers

A smaller problem which can confront investors is that of finding
themselves holding odd lots of shares, sometimes only one. This can
be a real nuisance: receiving reports, perhaps a couple of minuscule
dividends and costing more to sell than the holding is worth. This
situation can arise when a scrip issue arrives after the shares have
been sold.

A scrip issue usually gives the investor one new share for each share
held. It doubles the holding, halves the price and increases the share's
marketability without making any difference to the company except
perhaps to give it trustee status.

All that happens is a sum goes from reserves to issued share capital.
The issue makes no difference to investors except those who opted for
shares instead of dividends. After selling their shares (having ignored the
dividend date) they may receive a week or two later another one or two
shares as a scrip issue.

Whatever the reason for holding 'job lots' – inheritance, takeover,
even an emotional football share or two – there is a very good way of
getting rid of them which will create a warm glow in your heart without
making a hole in your pocket. You just give the odd lot(s) away to a
deserving charity. The medium for this transfer, which costs the
shareholder absolutely nothing, is ShareGift, the UK charity share
donation scheme.

ShareGift

ShareGift was launched in 1996 to provide a charitable home for
unwanted principally odd-lot shares. From a small beginning of £16,000
in its first year to £190,000 in the year 2000 it has already given away a
total of £600,000.

The largest gift so far is £50,000 but there have been hundreds of
small donations helped partly by income tax relief available on gifts to
charities.

Under the scheme, donated shares are re-registered and aggregated
until there are enough to sell. The current state of the market is not an

issue. Private client stockbrokers Killik & Co sell the shares for free and ShareGift's trustees then make charitable donations from the funds created in this way. All UK listed shares and some foreign holdings are accepted.

'Blue chip' companies (like BT, Marks & Spencer, Centrica, Rolls-Royce, P&O, Granada, BAe Systems, Lattice, Bass, BP Amoco, and Powergen) and UK building society windfall shares (such as Abbey National or Bradford and Bingley) are given frequently and soon add up to enough to sell. Gilts such as War Stock are also often donated, as are unit trust units, warrants and some loan notes.

Big companies sometimes add information about ShareGift in their annual reports or make a transfer form available through their registrars. This simplifies donations to many worthy charities. It is also possible to transfer odd lots from an online broker.

Investing overseas

Many of the larger UK broker firms deal in foreign equities, giving a wider choice of shares, and protection, via other currencies, against a possible fall in the pound. Direct deals through US brokers are comparatively cheap.

The USA offers a wide choice of shares, copious information on them, rapid execution speed and no stamp duty to pay. UK citizens must sign a certificate of foreign status of beneficial owner for United States Tax Withholding (Form W-8BEN).

To open an account with a US broker it is necessary to transfer US dollars from your own bank to an American bank through which the broker operates. The cost of doing this varies depending on the UK bank used, the speed required and the amount of the transaction. Interest is paid on accounts and the initial conversion cost is more than compensated by the cheapness of dealing.

The big danger however for anybody wanting to deal outside their own shores and not using a home-based broker (several of whom can deal for you) is the currency risk. A purchase of shares in a German 'blue chip' stock and held for two years to 2000 would have made a 35% gain which all dribbled away by the fall in the euro.

To avoid this scenario with the dollar, trade only in small sums. Cheap costs create larger profits.

Summary

To buy or sell shares contact a stockbroker, bank or financial adviser and choose an execution-only, advisory or discretionary service. This can be done by a personal visit to a financial institution, by phone, post, or the Internet. Go for the system with which you are most comfortable.

Phone dealing suits people who:
- have lots of patience and are not hard of hearing
- are in for the long haul and are prepared to wait for a good opportunity to buy or sell
- like their shares in paper form
- feel that phone dealing is safer and more private than having an online account
- want to deal through and change brokers without any hassle, real or perceived
- prefer to pay for their shares from their own bank accounts and do not mind waiting for cash when their shares are sold.

Online dealing suits people who:
- have a PC and are IT literate or can quickly become so
- know what shares they want and need no advice other than that which they can get from press news, books and Web sites
- have some spare cash to start and leave in their account
- like the opportunity of online chats
- do not mind the restriction of having only one broker
- want a speedy efficient dealing service
- want a quickly available record of their share transactions, including dividends/scrip issues received, current value of their portfolio and real-time share prices.

Chapter 7

Systems for success

"Nothing succeeds like success."
Proverb

What to buy; When to sell

HAVING SEEN how to buy and pay for shares, the next steps are what
to buy and when to sell. This chapter and those which follow, give details
of systems which are supposed to steer their practitioners into a land of
milk and honey. The innovators usually prosper. The disciples of the
systems more often fall into a quagmire by the wayside. See whether any
of the systems suit you. If not, go back to fundamental analysis. You
can't go far wrong if you buy a share with strong earnings growth, a
couple of other fundamentals and hold it for a few years.

Management

A system favoured by many financial institutions looking after the affairs
of their clients is to 'buy' management. The Alternative Investment
Market (AIM) may be the new place to search for tomorrow's
management 'winners'. In its early years, it spawned some 400
millionaire company founders and a new generation of managers is quite
likely to be found among that happy band.

Buying management rests on the idea that some people are so
dynamic that any company or organisation they head will always do
well. Napoleon used to ask of any general recommended to him, not
whether he was clever, talented, brilliant, brave, or whatever, but *"Is he
lucky?"* Whether the secret of managerial success is luck or judgement
or a combination of both, some individuals obviously have it.

Even during the huge shakeout of the electronics sector in the 1980s, the old General Electric Company (GEC) with Lord Weinstock at its head, came up with an eight per cent rise in profits to £725 million. Richard Giordano did wonders at the British Oxygen Company (BOC Group). Even more worthy of comment were his efforts at initiating training sessions for young people in computer technology. Not only do the early shareholders in his company have reason to be grateful to him, so do many of today's computer programmers.

Age is not a factor in management. At 76, Lord Forte lost none of the instinct and fighting spirit that enabled him to build up a chain of 800 hotels, worth around £1,000 million, from a capital base of just £1,400 and make the share price soar.

New products: the right entry point

One of the recommendations of William J O'Neill, (whose system How to Make Money in Stocks is described in a later chapter) is to buy, with certain reservations, shares in companies with new products. However, as many inventors and shareholders know to their cost, far from creating profits as one might expect, innovation and research can sometimes ring the death knell for previously profitable groups.

There are numerous examples. One only has to think of the 'black box' used for investigating air crashes. It perversely led to the demise of Royston Industries the company involved in its innovation and early production. The shares of pharmaceutical companies are particularly vulnerable to the acceptance or rejection of a newly-developed drug by the health authorities in the country to which the companies wish to export their wares. The thalidomide scandal never reached the dreadful proportions in the USA that it did in the UK because the US health authorities prevented its import.

Drugs and medical preparations often take years to create and finalise, during which time the company has to rely on its other products for profits. If the drug on which so much time, effort and money cannot pass the legislative health standards or proves later to have side effects, the shares will plummet.

If the drug is a success the shares will zoom. Zeneca (AstraZeneca), and Glaxo are examples of companies which spend millions on research and development in the hope of coming up with a cure for some currently intransigent disease.

Having seen the way that antibiotics are regarded almost as a cure-all for everything, I bought my first pharmaceutical share, Zeneca at £9. It now stands at around £30. I went into Wellcome too and would have held on, if I had not been persuaded by a doctor friend to sell. I went back into it years later when it was at the hugely high price of £15, but sold again when it went over £20.

By contrast a pharmaceutical company, which burgeoned into life on the AIM market and is now in the FTSE 350, has been unfortunate and so have I, in that every new 'cure' it has come up with somehow fails the last crucial test.

The right way to deal with perennial failures of this kind is to wait until an announcement is made of an impending trial. The share goes up fuelled by hope that this test will surely work. Sell then. If the trial goes badly, sit smugly on your profits; if it is successful, buy back the share when the market falls. You will have made a profit on your first sale, and can afford to wait for further growth.

Family fortunes

Another system used by some people, but less obvious today with so many conglomerates, is to target family businesses that go public. They often keep, for a generation at least, the creativity and dynamism of the original founders. One thinks of Salmon, Gluckstein and Joseph of Lyons, the Marks, Sieffs and Sachers of Marks and Spencer, and the Bulmer family of cider fame.

An interesting story of the Bulmer business was once told to me by a colleague, Nancy Cooke. Nancy, a brilliant lecturer of English, was one of the very few young women of her day to study at Cambridge under the great economist John Maynard Keynes. She happened also to be the granddaughter of the original founder of Bulmer and her story illustrates how an eventually big company can start up on a shoestring.

The label on Bulmer's first bottle of cider showed a rosy-cheeked maiden working with such modern machinery that a vigilant Tax Inspector thought that the business must be making (undisclosed) millions.

Hustling hotfoot to Hereford, the site of the head office, (the only office), he met the founder working in an unconverted byre. The conscientious inspector wondered what lay hidden behind this primitive set-up and asked to see the modern machinery. The proprietor, then owning only an apple orchard and a press, answered, *"We haven't bought it yet, but any day now…"*

The man from the Revenue, hurriedly hastened away, refusing the offer to meet the rosy-cheeked maiden. How right the proprietor's forecast was! Bulmer acquired many machines thereafter and went on to become a quoted public company with its share price veering between £4 and £5.

A somewhat different path was taken by Shelby Cullom Davis. By the time of his death in 1994 he was said to have made $900,million through investments. He left the money to a trust. His son and grandsons took over the running of the highly successful mutual funds business which he started on Wall Street. More about this remarkable financial dynasty and the system used by the founder, is outlined in chapter 11.

Another famous family which went public without losing its initial momentum for several years, were the Sainsburys. Employees were offered profit sharing in cash or shares seven years after the company came to the stock market. Those who took the shares saw them rise by 568 per cent.

Sainsbury's have inevitably lost ground since then to the big competitors like Walmart. This is another signal for those seeking stock market success by going for new management, new products, new ideas. Give the newcomers time to show their worth but look out for copycats. When they arrive, do not hang about. Get out, move on and bequeath the downturn to an investor who lacks your fleetness of foot. As Andrew Carnegie, the steel industry pioneer and philanthropist to many foundations, is purported to have said, "The first man gets the oyster, the second, the shell."

Vimto is a well-known UK non-alcoholic drink. The proprietors who started up the firm were a father and son. The importance of this relationship is emphasised in Forbes 400 lists. In the 1998 publication of self-made billionaires, all the businesses except Hallmark Cards were founded by male relatives.

Many executives have qualifications which appear to have little relevance to the industry in which they work. Accountants are increasingly appointed as managers even in industries such as railways where some knowledge of engineering might be expected.

By contrast, the 'junior' partner in Vimto the family business of father and sons had a chemistry degree which seemed very relevant to the drinks firm the family pioneered. When the firm started selling their drinks to the Muslim countries who are known for their non-addiction to alcohol, the share price went up. When top people know about the industry in which they work, and their organisation usually do very well. John White is an example. Starting life on a council estate and leaving school at 15, he began work as an apprentice bricklayer. This hardly seems the ideal beginning for a man who, for the past decade, has been at the helm of Persimmon, a house building business, with a market value of around £1 billion, at the last count. But having passed his bricklaying exams and taking a one day a week management course, he had learnt enough when he joined Persimmon in 1974 to get to the top. Housing can be a cyclical industry, and whether the company will go onwards or downwards and White with it, is a moot point. He remains optimistic.

Income seekers

A simple system for investors interested mainly in income would seem to be high yielders: companies or bonds paying bigger than average dividends. In economic climates of low interest rates, these usually compare very favourably with building society and bank deposit accounts. The advent of the millennium seemed an ideal time to begin.

Income from £1,000 invested in a typical UK building society account in 1990 fell from £105 to just £42 in 2001 and a £100,000 deposit then yielding a monthly income of £352 would have yielded £878 in 1990 (Source: *Standard & Poor's Micropal*). Rates for British savers in 2001 were at their lowest level since Disraeli was Prime Minister in 1874.

Yet income seekers found high yield bonds no help at all. In the USA, the economic slowdown, a deterioration in the credit quality of many companies, and the extreme volatility of the telecoms and technical companies which issued corporate bonds took their toll of many portfolios.

Europe was not immune. The Merrill Lynch European High Yield Bond index fell to 10.5% in June 2001 and was down 14.2% over the year to July 2001.

A better way in times of low growth and low interest rates is to buy not high yielding bonds, but high yielding shares. Like most 'simple' systems, this is not as easy as it sounds. Picking out companies paying good dividends takes comparatively little effort.

Choosing those that are not going to go belly up like a harpooned whale, needs a different approach.

When income is your objective, look for companies with strong, sustainable dividends. Do not ignore the overall aim of a good personal portfolio. A higher rate of income than is obtainable elsewhere appears attractive but not at the expense of growth.

Search for companies offering these two elements of income and growth and which are currently ignored by the investing community. If you can find such companies, be sure that eventually others will too, and the share price will soon go up. The early bird gets a double bonus, growth and income. Against a background of falling interest rates, such companies are particularly attractive.

To find them, begin with a computer program, magazine or newspaper, listing annual dividends per share. Among this group are companies paying dividends which give a yield at or above average for the sector or the particular index.

The figure shown will be the past dividend, one that has already been paid. It is not, unfortunately, a prediction for the future. It might also include special one-off payments to shareholders. This could give a false impression of the company's credit worthiness.

Don't go for dividends that stand out as particularly high, unless you enjoy wallowing in risk, for example, ten per cent might spell trouble ahead, unfavourable news in the wind or a fall in profits. Several companies in the list of high yielders, show a rate above the prevailing one.

More than seven per cent of the companies in the FTSE 350 often show yields higher than good deposit accounts. Look at the company's past profit record. Data and graphs are easily accessible. Check past dividend payouts. Have they grown over the past years, or is the present yield just a one-off due to some event which will be noted in the company reports? Allow for the fact that some companies need more cash for development plans, and so will pay miniscule dividends, or none at all.

Except for technology companies, where the practice is unfortunately fairly common, investors should regard with wariness and perhaps suspicion any passing of a dividend. If you are using a broker's advisory service, you might like at this stage to ask his opinion on the share/s you eventually choose. Does he think future payouts are likely to rise?

If the company is a small one, brokers may know as little about it as you, but they generally have more sources of information. Give your broker time and he will come back with an answer, likely to be hedged in by the customary caution of anybody giving advice.

Check the dividend cover for yourself. This is part of fundamental analysis although its calculation unfortunately varies from company to company. It shows the number of times the firm's net profits cover the dividend payment. Over 1% and under 5% make the best parameters. A share with a dividend yield of 5.59% covered 1.9 times and with no skeletons in the cupboard, should prove safe, sound and rewarding.

Stop loss system

Another method of picking the right share, which finds favour with some investors, is the stop loss system mentioned earlier. For the most basic type of stop loss, you pick two points above and below the buying price of your share. It can be ten per cent or more each way. Allowing for your overall costs might mean a higher amount like 20 per cent. Make up your own mind about the target that suits you.

Example: The stop loss system

You buy a share costing 100p. Your upper point is 120 and your lower one is 80. If the share price reaches either of those points you sell. This basic stop loss approach can cause you to miss maximum profits on a share that is rising with a few hiccups on the way, but it also saves you from disastrous losses.

A more sophisticated example of the stop loss system is to raise the stakes. In other words, if the share price reaches 120, you move your stop loss point up 20 per cent of 120 to 144. At 144 it goes up another 20 per cent and so on. You sell when the price falls 20 per cent below the new peak. So at the peak of 144 the selling price would be 20 per cent of that figure, or a little over 115.2. This system ensures you never miss out on a profit, but never get the best.

The hatch system

The hatch system is similar to the trailing stop loss system in that it works on a ratchet. Again a figure of, say, ten per cent is attached to any profit or loss you make which similarly may lose you some profit on the upside, but safeguards you from slipping into the country of no return. In this way, you can still be the winner in the pack by losing the smallest possible amount when you are wrong.

The system can be used for an index, an individual share or a group of shares. When a group of leading shares are chosen, they are likely to move in line with the market. This is somewhat like a tracker fund and gives the portfolio the benefit of averaging. Sometimes averages are used for the previous week or month instead of a single price on a fixed date. In all cases, the automatic signals must be obeyed.

The hatch or trailing loss system (TLS) is meant for long-term investment, not speculation, and its advantages are that losses are limited to an adjustable ten per cent of the amount invested. It prevents selling out too soon in a long bull market, or buying too early in a bear market. One danger point is that if markets move narrowly for a long time, an investor could be going in and out with a series of small losses.

To show a profit using ten per cent as the trailing loss, the market has to rise by more than 22.2 per cent so the system does best in a rising market. Thus if the bottom line is rated at 100, the share is bought at 110. (TLS ten per cent above). Unless the market rises to 122.2 when an investor's selling price will be 110 (122.2 – 12.2) no gain is made.

Example: The hatch system

On 1st August, an investor buys a share for $1.70 and deducts ten per cent from the price ($1.70 – $0.17 = $1.53) to establish an automatic selling price. If the price at any time falls to $1.53 he immediately sells the share. If the price rises above the actual purchase price of $1.70, he deducts ten per cent to establish a new selling price.

On 1st September the share stands at $1.69. The investor does nothing because the price has not fallen below $1.53, nor risen above $1.70.

On 1st October the price of the share rises to $1.84, higher than the actual purchase price of $1.70. Ten per cent is deducted ($1.84 – $0.18 = $1.66) so that $1.66 is the new price replacing $1.53, at which the share was to be sold.

On 1st November the share price rises to $2.25. As this is higher than the 1st October price, a new selling price is established ($2.25 – $0.23 = $2.03).

On 1st December the share price is $2.10. As this is lower than the November price of $2.25, but higher than $2.03 no adjustment is made.

On 1st January the price falls to $2.03, and the share is sold.

Volume spread analysis

Some successful investors swear that volume (the number of shares traded on a particular day) and price are the keys to success. One such advocate of this idea in the UK is Tom Williams. He has greatly profited by using it, selling the software program (VSA7) he has devised and arranging seminars to explain the system. His disciples are enthusiastic, as are his customers, but a little time must be given to it daily, so in this regard, it may be more helpful to short-term traders than long-term investors.

In Volume Spread Analysis, the only volume to be considered is that created by financial institutions. The content of a large program like VSA7 cannot be digested quickly but its essence is that when a low share price is accompanied by low volume, this means that none of the institutions are selling, even at this low price. When an upward curve to the share price begins, this presents a buying opportunity. If a high price is accompanied by low volume, the buying price is exhausted: time to sell.

The CANSLIM approach

William J O'Neill began trading with the purchase of just five shares in Proctor & Gamble when he was 21 and fresh out of school. He is now the founder of *Investor's Business Daily* and the author of *How to Make Money in Stocks*. He propounds "a winning system in good times or bad" and calls it the CANSLIM approach. This is a mnemonic for a series of tips to help improve investment returns. They are developed and expanded throughout his book. In brief they are:

- C for current quarterly earnings per share. These should show a major increase compared with the previous year's same quarterly earnings.
- A for annual earnings. Look for an increase per share over the past five years.
- N for new. The investor must buy, *at the right time,* new products, new management, new highs. (Some of these have been mentioned above in the paragraph on the right entry point.)
- S is for supply and demand: small capitalisation plus big volume demand. (Tom Williams' approach on volume analysis does not involve capitalisation. Smaller issues will always do

better, percentage wise, than larger ones. The important point is which one gives the bigger profit?)

- **L** is for the question 'leader or laggard?' The 'laggard' approach is sometimes used by analysts who suggest that buying last year's 'losers' will perform better in an upturn of the market than last year's winners, the 'leaders' in the pack. There is no logical reason why they should. Au contraire.
- **I** is for institutional sponsorship (see below).
- **M** is for market direction (see below).

Notes on the CANSLIM system

O'Neill defines 'L', a laggard, by looking at the stock's relative price strength on a scale from 1 to 99. If it is below 70, that stock is lagging the better performing stocks in the overall market. If you must restrict your purchases, choose only the chart-based companies showing a relative strength of 80 or higher.

Relative price strength compares the price of a stock with the market average of, for example, the S & P index. A relative strength of 70 means a stock outperformed 70% of the standard stocks in the comparison group during a given period, say the last six or twelve months.

You usually have to pay for figures and charts showing relative strength numbers. Excellent software packages are available which give these daily for all the listed stocks in the New York Stock Exchange (NYSE), AMEX (American Stock Exchange) and NASDAQ price tables.

'I' for institutional sponsorship has only minor relevance for UK investors. The London Stock Exchange instituted a new system from midsummer 2001. This corrects the rating of companies where too large a percentage of the share in issue is owned by one group, institution or sponsor so giving it a capitalisation which does not reflect accurately the public's holding of the shares. The new system removing these holdings from the shares' capitalisation figure, gives a fairer assessment of the company's real worth. The so-called 'free float' restrictions include trade investments in an index constituent; significant long-term holdings by founders, their families and/or directors; employee share schemes (if restricted); Government holdings; foreign ownership limits and portfolio investment subject to a lock-in clause, for the duration of that clause.

'M' for market direction is perhaps too ambitious for the average investor. There are too many indicators to check, although the theory is simple enough, namely to know whether you are in a bull market going up or a bear market going down. O'Neill recommends looking at historical data and following the general market averages every day. This advice is more suited to the short-term trader than the long-term investor.

Systems for 'winning' losers

Get out at the top is a truism known even to the novice investor, but finding it? …there's the rub. If you hang about, the market floods down. If you've borrowed to deal on margin, you are swept away in the avalanche. Some analysts concentrate on what might seem a more negative approach: strategies to avoid losing. This is perhaps one way of successful investing, particularly important for those who want to save for their retirement.

It is epitomised by Charles D. Ellis's approach which he first propounded under the title *The Losers' Game*. This followed Nobel Laureate Paul Samuelson's classic article *Challenge to Judgment*. From these beginnings came the very first index mutual funds. Today, there are many other indices which help investors in their judgements and comparisons.

The theme which Charles Ellis takes up is that many investors, Americans especially, are making significant errors in planning for their retirement, (1) by owning, without strategic aims, too many mutual funds, (2) by being too conservative in their investment decisions for the long term, (3) by being too dependent on owning company stock rather than shares, and (4) by not giving enough attention to fees and expenses without appreciating that, in the long run, cost matters. John Bogle in his introduction, does not recommend selling the family farm to buy equities, but highlights the faults outlined with some figures.

Example: 'Winning' losers

Assume investment costs at 4.5 per cent for cash and 7.5 per cent for stocks. John Doe saves $300 per month in a retirement plan, thus investing $90,000 over 25 years. At the end of that time, a portfolio of 30 reserves / 70 stocks would produce a retirement fund of $283,000, while a high cost portfolio of 70 reserves / 30 stocks would produce a fund of $190,000: a reduction of nearly $100,000.

The arithmetic may alter, but the message remains the same: the value of being less risk-averse to the value of equities. I endorse this idea until the last 5–10 years of a retirement plan, whatever it may be called, and go for something with very little risk indeed. You are unlikely to collect any laurels, bonuses or salary increases after the age of 65, and even if you are, you might as well be safe as sorry.

The other two messages from what might be called the winning loser's guide, is firstly to avoid emotion in any investment strategy, and secondly, is the value of simplicity in investing, that is do not have too many mutual funds (unit trusts) or trade too often, going from one speculative fund to another. In other words, the catchphrase is KISS – keep it simple, stupid.

Simple systems

Simple systems often give the best results. Some examples are selling half your shares when they have made a profit acceptable to you, and keeping half; looking up the best sector and choosing the best stock in that group; going for a stock because you work in the company and know its virtues (as did William O'Neill); going for a company because you know and like its products; ...and if you're going into bonds, watch the trend of interest rates and hope that if you're not clever, you may, like Napoleon's generals, be lucky until the last battle when you switch sides and become luckier still.

Summary

If you do not want to choose fundamentals or to chart patterns for your investment portfolio, there are many other systems that promise a financial Eden. Know your aims and time span in which you want to achieve them. Avoid acting on impulse or emotion, and when you've found a system that suits you, one that appears relatively risk free and is sound and simple, use and hold on to it.

Chapter 8

Technical analysis

*"You don't want analysts in a bear market
and you don't need them in a bull market."*
Gerald M. Loeb

Trading or investing?

THERE ARE some investors who act like soothsayers when confronted with charts. These wonderful patterns, they assert, are the route to a personal fortune. Study them and you too will join 'THE RICH'. It is true that much can be learned from charts. Some famous investors and managers rely on little else. Charts show aspects of shares which cannot be gleaned so quickly or clearly by looking at figures or other data.

Volume can be seen at a glance; so can the highs and lows of a particular share on any given day or over a period of time. Charts show turning points when a share starts to climb up and the reverse indicator when they start a downward trend.

Yet in spite of all the advantages that these patterns bring, there are probably only a certain number that are really worthy of consideration.

Furthermore, the majority of technical analysts do not believe in the buy and hold approach to investing. Not for them is the tucking away of spare cash into a share or unit trust (mutual fund), to be treated like a vestal virgin, untouchable until some date far in the future.

They assert that stock markets have undergone a revolution since the 1980s and 1990s with a volatility that may alter prices by 20–25% in a day. Some stocks triple in a week and their prices halve in a fortnight. This volatility, so the 'technicians' claim, can lead to huge profits without waiting over two generation for them. Ed Downs, in his book *7 Chart Patterns That Consistently Make Money*, illustrates this point by showing a chart of Ethan Allen.

In this example, an investor purchasing the share in January 1998 and holding it for one year to January 1999 would have realised a 13% gain. However, by selling the stock in April 1998, a 45% gain would have been made. Selling and buying as the stock declined in the summer months would have added another 46%, and a purchase in early October would have yielded 68% by January 1999. To achieve results like this the trader has to know the right entry and exit points (as well as some good 'discount' brokers who will not charge the earth for a trade). These vital points, so it is claimed, can be found by using technical analysis.

Definition

The system sounds complicated. Bared to the bone, it is actually very simple: the study of prices with charts as the main tool. The system has a good heritage having been developed more than a century ago by Charles Dow (perhaps more famous in another context – the Dow Jones Industrial Average index in the USA). He initiated a new way of looking at changes in stock market prices and so can be regarded as the forerunner of modern-day technical analysis. Many of his theories such as price trends, volume (reflecting changes in price), confirmation and divergence, are still used today.

Yet in spite of this brilliant and innovative father figure, the apparent simplicity of the system and its numerous adherents, two big hurdles confront any investor trying to use it as a means of jumping off into profit. They are (a) knowing the tools, and (b) how to interpret them.

There is another downside. If you think technical analysis will tell you what price your share will be tomorrow, next week, or next year, my own cynical advice is, think again. It is easy to grow rich when you know the answers, but who does? Technical analysts think they do. That may well be true: the proof of the pudding is in the eating.

What can be proved is that understanding technical analysis certainly increases knowledge of the share markets and helps investors to make logical choices instead of being fogged by the miasma of fear, panic and greed. It also shows trend lines: the way a stock appears to be moving, so that even if you can't predict actual future prices, you get a good idea of where they are going.

Differences

Technical analysts compare the current price of a stock with historical ones so as to determine its probable future price, a kind of history repeating itself approach. By contrast, fundamental analysts try to determine the value of a stock by looking at the key statistics in companies' reports and similar data. They predict future price movements on the basis of these fundamentals and by deciding whether or not the current price correctly mirrors the right value.

If it does not, the price should move up or down. What should happen, however, does not always do so because human expectations change. They are not easily quantifiable nor predictable. Any system, say the 'technicians', which does not take this fact into account is doomed to failure. It could only work if humans were logical creatures who separated their emotions from their investment decisions.

Continuing the supposition of completely logical human beings, in such an environment everybody would have the same expectations, and so prices could change only after the receipt of relevant reports or news. The only gainers would be those investors searching (successfully) amongst the data for undervalued securities.

One of the proven advantages of technical analysis and which gives the system an edge over its 'rivals' is the computer software that comes up with such excellent charts and graphs. Many of these programs are extremely powerful tools for all kinds of investors, not only those wedded to technical analysis.

Although cynics allege that it is not possible, even with the most perfect aids, to know with absolute precision, the future price of a stock, this should not deter the beginner investor. The aim of the game is to improve the odds in the player's favour. That is more likely to happen even if the analysis used only determines the long-, intermediate and short-term trends of a stock.

Systems, whether dependent on mechanical means, knowledge, experience or intuition, are meant to lead to profitable returns, but tools are only as good as their users. Author Steven B. Achelis puts out a warning note, "...since we are analysing a less than logical subject (human emotions and expectations), we must be careful that our mechanical systems don't mislead us into thinking that we are analysing a logical entity. In my totally biased opinion, technical analysis software has done more to level the playing field for the average investor than any other non-regulatory event. But as a provider of technical analysis tools,

I caution you not to let the software lull you into believing markets are as logical and predictable as the computer you use to analyze them."

So before diving into the technical analyst's tool kit, remember that no matter how ingenious the tools may be that you find there, if you do not profit from their use, they will prove as helpful to you as a suet pudding to a person wanting to slim.

Tools

The two major tools in the analyst's cornucopia, are price and volume. The terms that define them are briefly explained below.

- **Open** is especially important for daily data. It is the price of the first trade of the day or whatever other period is being studied. The importance of this figure is that it is reached after all interested parties have had time to reflect on it.
- **High** is the highest price at which the stock traded during the period being scrutinised. At this point there are more sellers than buyers.
- **Low** is the lowest price at which the security traded in the period being surveyed. At this point there are more buyers than sellers.
- **Close** is the last trading price of the period, the figure considered significant by analysts and most often used by them.
- **Volume** indicates the number of shares (or contracts) traded during the period. The relationship between prices and volume is one of the most important in technical analysis. This is particularly so when increasing prices are accompanied by increasing volume.
- **Open Interest** gives the total number of outstanding contracts. These apply to futures and options and those that are still open, have not expired, been exercised, or closed.
- **Bid** is the price received if you sell.
- **Ask** is the price you pay to buy the share.

These simple fields can create hundreds of tools for the study of price relationships, trends, patterns and so on, although not all of the fields are available for all security types. The table below shows different security types: stocks, mutual funds, futures, and options, and typical fields used by them.

	FUTURES	MUTUAL	FUNDS	STOCKS
Open	Yes	No	Often	Yes
High	Yes	Closed end	Yes	Yes
Low	Yes	Closed end	Yes	Yes
Close	Yes	Yes (*NAV)	Yes	Yes
Volume	Yes	Closed end	Yes	Yes
Open int	Yes	N/A	N/A	Often
Bid	Intraday	Closed end	Intraday	Intraday
Ask	Intraday	Closed end	Intraday	Intraday

*Net Asset Value.   *Source: Technical Analysis: Steven B. Achelis*

Charts

Charts show the analyst's tools in graphic form. Those relating to price are typically drawn in one of two styles: line or bar. The number of transactions in a days' trading are shown in volume bars.

Line charts

Line charts are the simplest. They consist of a single line joining up the stock's closing price each day. Days or other periods of time are shown on the horizontal axis, prices on the vertical axis.

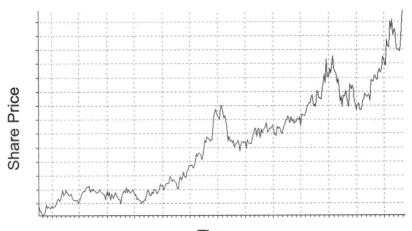

Bar charts

Bar charts are the most popular. They give high, low and closing prices. Each price bar is shown as a vertical line from the high to low; the top represents the highest price in the day or relevant period; the bottom represents the lowest. A tiny horizontal tick on the left side of the bar indicates the share's opening price, a similar tick on the right, the closing price. Neither need be the highest or lowest.

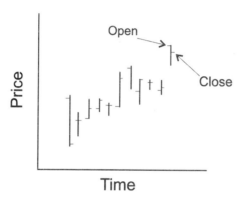

Volume bar chart

When volume is displayed, it is usually at the bottom of the chart and in one of two ways, either zero related where the volume starts from zero; or relative adjusted which analysts prefer. The latter deducts the lowest figure for the period from all the volume bars equally, so that the big trends are more easily seen.

Candlestick charts

Candlestick charts were developed by the Japanese in the seventeenth-century to monitor the price of rice contracts. When used today, they illustrate supply and demand by displaying the open, low, high and closing prices in a format similar to a bar chart. Focusing on the relationship between the first price (the Open) and the last price (the Close), makes them useful to many types of investors.

The interpretation of the charts rests on their patterns: bullish, bearish, reversal or neutral. The names given to the patterns indicate what they are meant to represent. The format involves no calculations and represents one period, for example a day or week of trading. In a candlestick chart, the range between the open and close is shown as a filled-in rectangle, or body when the closing price is lower than the opening price; an open rectangle when the closing price is higher than the opening.

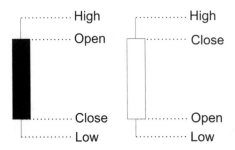

Point and figure

Point and Figure differs from all the other technical analysis charts in that (a) it ignores the time element, and (b) it displays only prices on both axes. The function of this kind of chart is to show the underlying supply and demand of prices. A column of Os shows an excess of supply (prices falling), while a column of X's show demand exceeding supply (prices rising).

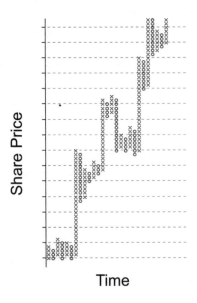

Price changes

The points on a graph which show where prices stop falling or rising are known as the support and resistance levels. The changes arise because investor expectations alter, perhaps because of changes in the management of a company, in its earnings or in its profit forecasts.

Support levels occur when it is expected that the price will not move lower. Resistance levels are those points where a falling price is halted and goes no lower because resistance is met from buyers. Volume helps determine the strength of that resistance and support.

Support/resistance levels

The price of any stock represents the fair market value agreed between buyers and sellers. It changes when investors expect it to.

Support levels occur when the price will not move lower and resistance levels occur when it will not move higher.

Change in support or resistance levels indicate a change in investor expectations and of supply and demand for the stock.

Volume helps to show the strength of the change of expectations.

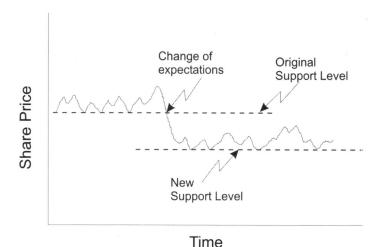

Trends

Trends are an important element in technical analysis. Unlike support/resistance levels which show barriers to change, trends show the direction of the change. A rising trend has a support level with successively higher 'low' prices. A falling trend has a resistance level with successively lower 'high' prices: so the resistance level is also going down.

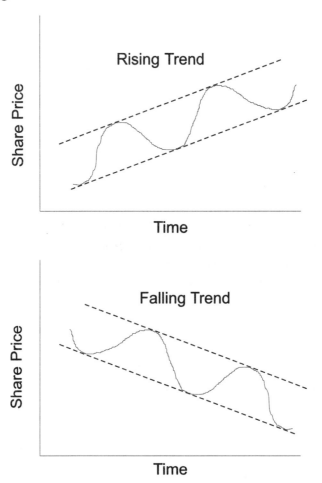

Moving averages

If you are not impressed with technical analysis and think it is a form of being wise after the event, at least look at a stock's moving average. The average price of a security at a given time, is one of the oldest and most popular technical analysis tools around and often used for observing price changes in a share price at a given time.

To calculate it you must specify the time span, for example 30 days. You add together the prices of the stock for the most recent 30 days and then divide by 30. That gives you the share's average price over the last 30 days. The next day, you perform the same calculation using the latest 30 days price data (meaning the oldest data point will have dropped out of the average, being now 31 days ago, and the most recent will be included).

When the security's price is above its moving average, investors' current expectations are higher than their average expectations over the last 30 days. They are becoming more optimistic about the stock. When today's price is below its moving average, current expectations are below the average expectations over the last 30 days. Investors usually buy when the price is above its moving average, and sell when it falls below. Ignoring commission charges, the biggest profits are usually obtained during short time periods.

Pros and cons

If you buy and sell when prices penetrate their moving average, you will always be on the right side of the market. Prices cannot rise very much without the price rising above its average price. However the disadvantage of this system is that you will always buy and sell late. If the trend doesn't last for a significant period of time, typically twice the length of the moving average you'll lose some of your cash.

You can get long-term trends in a stock by using a longer period such as 200 days for a moving average. Some computer software shows the number of time periods to give the optimum result.

One proven variant on the theme of moving averages is to use 10- and 30-day time periods. Having bought a particular stock, stick with it, no matter what the other indicators show, as long as the 10-day average is above the 30-day one. Only sell when the 10-day average falls below the 30-day average.

Indicators

A moving average is an indicator, a calculation which is used to anticipate future price changes. All of the many indicators in use are designed to do just that. An often used relatively simple indicator is the Moving Average Convergence Divergence (MACD).

To find it, you subtract the 12-day moving average of a share price from its 26-day moving average. The resulting indicator oscillates above and below zero. When the MACD is above zero, the 12-day average will be above the 26-day one, so the omens are good. Expectations are higher than previously. When the MACD falls below zero, the current 12-day moving average is lower than the previous 26, showing a shift downwards in demand for the stock relative to its supply.

A nine-day moving average of the MACD is usually plotted on top of the MACD indicator. It is known as the 'signal' line because it anticipates the movement of the MACD towards the zero line, that is, where the two moving averages converge.

Leading and lagging indicators

Moving averages and the MACD lag, that is follow rather than make trends. Showing graphically whether prices are rising or falling, they are excellent tools for prices which move over relatively long periods. 'Let the trend be your friend,' it is sometimes said and if you follow lagging indicators, you are unlikely to lose your money. You will however be investing after the leaders in the pack. Prices will have gone up or down by the time you enter the market. You won't make top profits, but neither will you make the biggest losses.

By contrast, leading indicators, unlike the lagging ones, predict what prices will do next. In this way they offer greater rewards against the chance of greater risk. When the trend of a security's price does not agree with an indicator's trend, this is known as a divergence. At that point prices tend to change direction, confirming the indicator's trend.

Market indicators

All the technical analysis tools described so far are used to calculate expected prices of an individual share. They are limited to its open, high, low, close and volume. To gauge changes within a specific market, such as the FTSE or Dow, you need market indicators. They survey not just one stock but the whole market and contain much more information than price and volume. They show, for example, the number of stocks making new highs for the day, the volume of stocks that increased in price and other data. Much of this is probably more helpful to traders dealing in futures and other derivatives than to the average investor.

Anybody using market indicators to determine where the overall market is heading should follow this up by price/volume indicators. These signal when to buy or sell an individual share. Whether the market is rising or falling, the extra signal is likely to double your chances of profit and minimise your chances of loss. There are three basic types of market indicators: monetary, sentiment, and momentum.

Monetary indicators

These concentrate on economic data which affect the environment of business operations, their profits and ultimately their share price. Such data can include interest or exchange rates, the money supply, consumer/corporate debt and inflation. It shows what share prices should do *(Be Warned*: In this regard, prices are like children - what they should do is not always what they actually do).

Sentiment

This second market indicator, like an abstruse article for a limited readership of academics, completely ignores the expectations of the average investor and offers such esoteric fare as the put/call ratio (how many people are buying 'puts' versus 'calls'), premiums on stock index futures or the ratio of 'bullish' versus 'bearish' investment advisers.

There is one concession to Joe Average. It was once said that anybody who travelled on a No. 35 London bus after the age of 30 was not a success in life. If any of these travellers still exist, the concession they get in the sentiment market indicator could switch them from their bus seat to a Mercedes or stretch limo. This magic transmuter is the contrarian approach, often used by successful fund managers.

There are two ways of being a 'contrarian'. One is to buy the share that has fallen most during the past year in an index such as the FTSE 100 (a dangerous ploy which might have you put off the bus for not paying the fare). The second is to do the opposite of what the majority of investors expect. If they expect prices to rise the contrarian sells, preferably at near market peaks, and buys at the bottom when everybody else is selling. As investors tend to buy on a rising market and sell when the market has nearly reached bottom, the contrarian approach may work.

Momentum

The third category of market indicator is momentum. This covers a whole spectrum of data such as the MACD of the Dow Industrials, numbers of new low and high comparisons of price, and volume. The object is to show not what prices might be expected to do but what prices are actually doing.

Popular graph patterns

Other tools popular with technical analysts are the graph patterns of double tops and double bottoms, names often bandied about among experienced traders, although with what profit it is difficult to say. A double top occurs when on significant volume, prices rise to a resistance level. They fall back and return later to the resistance level on decreased volume. Prices then fall again to begin a new downtrend. A double bottom has the same characteristics but shows a reverse (upside down) pattern on the chart. This illustrates a double top with low volume – a sell signal.

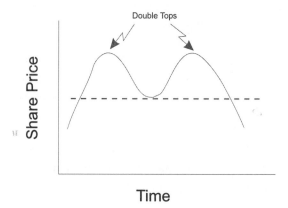

The investors' conundrum

From such a variety of investment analysis tools on offer, how does the ordinary investor in shares begin? One answer is to look at trends and interest rates. The trend in investor sentiment, also necessary to know, can be gauged from newspaper reports. Choose a stock about which you know something: its price over the past years, manager, product, or rely on your broker if you are using a discretionary service. The next stage is harder. Plot a long-term moving average (200 days or 39 weeks) and a good buying signal is when the stock has just risen above this average. Alternatively try the 10- and 30-day averages already mentioned in the section on Moving averages.

Resistance levels give clues when to sell. A very simple system which can do no harm is if a share price goes up by at least 40%, sell half. This reduces potential profit, but come what may, the rest of the share is in for free. Whether you prefer the fundamental or technical approach, or a mixture of both, the use of steps outlined in this chapter will help to lessen risks and maximise the opportunities for gain.

Warnings

Don't
- buy more of the same at lower prices (averaging down only compounds a loss),
- hold on to a share if you would not buy it now,
- be impressed by the apparent investment success of others,
- maximise risks or waste opportunities.

Short- or long-term

The main question to consider when deciding whether or not to use technical analysis or any of its many tools, is are you going to be a long-term investor or short-term trader, that is one who comes in and out as the opportunities for buying and selling present themselves? There are advantages and disadvantages in both stances. If you are thinking about joining the short-term investors who are more like traders, then the following maths lesson may be useful. It is not a tool of technical analysis but an illustration of the returns possible by short-term trading. The example may be helpful to older readers or those of an impatient nature who cannot afford to wait for twenty years to see their assets grow.

Quick maths lesson

By averaging 1% profit on every deal you make, you could show at the end of the year a return of 38.9% on a 100% invested position, …but only if you are on your toes.

The average position that is buying or selling turns in 7.5 market days. There are 252 market days in a year, 252 / 7.5 = 33.6 turns per year. The annual return is calculated as follows:

Annual return on investment (ROI) =
1.01 raised to the 33rd power −1 =
[(1.01 x 1.01 x 1.01 x 1.01 x 1.01 x 1.01 x 1.01 x 1.01 x 1.01 x 1.01 x
1.01 x 1.01 x 1.01x 1.01 x 1.01 x 1.01 x 1.01 x 1.01 x 1.01 x 1.01 x
1.01 x 1.01 x 1.01 x 1.01 x 1.01 x 1.01 x 1.01 x 1.01 x 1.01 x 1.01 x
1.01x 1.01 x 1.01) - 1] x 100 = 38.9%

This table shows the Annual ROI calculated by different average trading.

Average / trade	Annual ROI
0.5%	17.9%
1.0%	38.9%
1.5%	63.4%
2.0%	92.2%
2.5%	125.9%

Against these facts you might like to ponder the words of author Burton Malkiel. In the seventh edition of his book *A Random Walk down Wall Street*, he writes, *"The central proposition of charting is absolutely false, and investors who follow its precepts will accomplish nothing but increasing substantially the brokerage charges they pay. There has been a remarkable uniformity in the conclusions of studies done on all forms of technical analysis. Not one has consistently outperformed the placebo of a buy-and-hold strategy."* So there you have two sides of the coin. Perhaps fundamental analysis holds the key to investment wealth?

Summary

Technical analysis is the study of prices and volume using charts as the main tool. Resistance and support levels give clues to future prices with buy and sell signals shown by breakouts or reversals.

Chapter 9

Fundamental analysis

"...don't do equations with Greek letters in them."
Warren Buffett

Fundamental and technical analyses

FUNDAMENTAL AND technical analysis, both focus on the prices of shares. These are of obvious importance to the investor (else why invest at all?) so it is worthwhile looking at the two systems. What do they offer? Have their disciples the Midas touch and, better still, can they pass it on to others?

The 'technicians' use charts to find the best entry or exit point for a particular share or index. Having found it, they compare this price with the preceding ones. The object of their search is to discover trends or expectations which determine the future path of the share or index. This kind of history repeating itself approach helps technical analysts decide the right time to buy and sell.

By contrast, the 'fundamentalists' concentrate on the best company in which to invest. Having found one that appears suitable, they search for confirmation of its intrinsic worth in reports, accounts and similar data. This information helps them, and other interested parties, to assess whether the share price accurately reflects that worth. So the basic difference between the two systems of analysis is that fundamentalists focus on **what** and the technicians on **when** to buy and sell.

After seeing, what might be called in today's jargon, its vital statistics, the fundamental analysts then go further afield. They look at economic, industry and company information to check whether their findings about the company need to be altered in the light of this additional knowledge. Does the share price accurately mirror the company's true value?

Perhaps prompted by a touch of professional malice, the technicians allege that their own charts make investors aware of what is actually happening in the market while fundamental analysis merely informs as to what should happen and never does.

For good measure, the technicians remind us that there are other problems with fundamentals. Firstly, they can be difficult to quantify. When a company dreams up a new product, it may seem to be a winner, but the proof of its success will only be apparent when it is actually produced and sold.

Secondly, while technical analysis lends itself to rapid, automated processing by a computer, fundamental analysis does not. Even if this were strictly true, it need not be a disadvantage. There sometimes seem almost as many software programs for technicians as shares in the market. But fundamentalists do not rely solely on the lowly calculator to discover the figures they need and the calculations of ratios they wish to make. They too, can access the computer to augment the information found in company accounts.

Thirdly, fundamental factors are often 'discounted' in the market.

This is seen when a company produces a very good earnings report and yet its share price falls. What has happened is that too many people, aware of the company's forthcoming good news, have bought into the share. The price goes up, the early bird flies off with the worm, the results are published and the price falls. The market is reassessing the shares in the light of the next results, not reflecting the present ones. There are other reasons why results do not always seem to be mirrored in the share price, for example the company:

- has trouble looming ahead,
- is too small to interest pension, mutual and other big investing funds,
- is a good one but the sector is currently in the doldrums.

In spite of these apparent disadvantages, some investors, including fund managers, swear by fundamentals because they cover not only the quantifiable but the non-quantifiable indications of a company's worth. These include earnings and earnings growth, book value, market share, insider trading statistics, new products and new markets.

If you want to find shares with excellent growth prospects compounded by their earnings, then fundamental analysis is a must, because figures don't lie, or so it is said, and the trend of past earnings at least, are there for all to see.

The analysts focus on the share which in their opinion gives the best returns. Considering the number of shares in the UK market alone, that is a formidable task. Even if the 3000 or so are whittled down to the best 350, it still takes some doing. This is why fundamentalists bring other factors into the equation, such as economic conditions, including interest, exchange and inflation rates. Will they rise or fall?

Economic conditions

What about the money supply: are people saving or spending? Private investors, unlike economists or fund managers, are not privy to all this information, but can get a good idea of the economic climate in a country at any given time.

They are aware of the employment situation, particularly if their jobs are on the line. Travels abroad allow them to compare price levels with those at home, even if rising prices don't reveal the exact level of inflation. These facts and their impact on a company are worth looking at when considering its inclusion in a particular portfolio.

Industry conditions

Fundamentalists study industry conditions because they affect companies in different ways. If storm clouds are brewing owing to strikes or a period of bad industrial relations, some industries will weather them; others crumble under the deluge. Even the most efficient firms are likely to announce mediocre results in such a climate.

Company analysis

This type of analysis studies the company's report and statement of accounts, sent out half-yearly to shareholders. Other interested parties can get the report and facts about the company from the company itself, its Registrar, or, in the UK, from Companies House. The material helps in assessing the company's financial health. It also provides the basis for calculations of useful ratios.

By comparing these ratios with those of other companies in the same or similar industry, an idea is obtained of what might be regarded as 'normal' for the sector. The ratios fall into five main categories: profitability, price, liquidity, leverage, and efficiency. Some popular

examples in each category are shown below. They are worth a glance –
investing your money without investing your time lessens your chance
of profit and maximises your chance of loss.

Profitability

Investors in a company naturally want to find out how much profit it
makes. Ignore the deceptive gross profit figure. That does not tell you
how much was spent to get that profit. Net profit margin is the total to
look for: the after sales money that actually returns to the company. It is
shown by the profitability ratio, a truly lovely concept found by dividing
net income by total sales. This ratio indicates how much profit the
company can squeeze out of each dollar of sales. As an example, if a
company has a net profit margin of 35 per cent, then $0.35 of every $1
in sales comes back in profits.

Earnings per share (EPS)

The total net profit made by the company after tax and all other
deductions, is a clue to another vital statistic: earnings per share (EPS).
The net profit divided by the number of shares, gives the earnings on
each share. For fundamentalists, EPS is one of the most important
components of stock selection. The size of the increase or decrease
matters less than the trend. Is the EPS going up or down?

In his book, *How to Make Money in Stocks*, William O'Neill quotes
his study over the period 1953–1993 of the 500 best performing stocks.
Seventy-five per cent of them showed EPS increases averaging more than
70% in the immediate published figures before a major price advance.
The 25% that showed no increase, did so even more spectacularly in the
next quarter. The message for investors, fundamentalists or not, is to
check earnings of shares that they 'fancy', which have come to their
notice or been found in one of the indices, put the best into a file to be
watched, and at the right moment, sought and bought.

Price/Earnings ratio

The Price/Earnings (P/E) ratio shows how much an investor pays to
'buy' $1 of a company's earnings. Investor expectations of a company's
future performance play an important role in this figure. To find it, take

the share's current price and divide it by the annual earnings per share (EPS). If a stock's current price is, say, $20 and the EPS for the last four quarters was $2, the P/E ratio is 10 ($20/2). You are paying $10 to 'buy' $1 of the company's earnings.

The P/E falls when a company's annual earnings increase. The share price then looks cheap. Buyers flood in. The share price will rise to the more normal level for the industry.

Fundamental analysts regard the P/E ratio as an important indicator in a particular share. By contrast, the technical analysts will watch the increased volume of buyers and the upward trend of the share price, possibly using a computer program. Other things being equal, the company with the lower P/E ratio is the better value.

Jim Slater, author of *Beyond the Zulu Principle*, goes one better than the P/E ratio. Useful though this is, he stresses that it is a one-dimensional measure.

More meaningful, he suggests, is the relationship between the P/E ratio and its expected rate of earnings per share growth. He calls this 'invaluable investment tool', the price earnings growth (PEG) factor. It is a prime ingredient of his criteria for selecting growth shares to beat the market. In his mandatory list he includes a PEG with a relatively low cut-off, such as 0.75, and also a prospective P/E ratio of not more than 20. The preferred range for P/E ratios is 10–20 with forecast growth rates of 15–30%.

Book value per share

A company's book value is its net assets. From this figure (assets minus liabilities) comes another useful price ratio: total assets divided by the number of shares. Depending on the accounting methods used and the age of the assets, book value can be helpful in determining whether a share is overpriced or not. If the price is far below book value, the security is underpriced and vice versa.

Current ratio

A company's current ratio is a liquidity ratio, in other words what cash or near-cash the company has with which to meet its debts. It is found by dividing current liabilities into current assets. The reason for assessing this ratio is that the result provides investors (and other interested parties such as auditors and creditors) with a measure of the company's ability to meet its current debts. The higher the ratio, the more liquid the company. For example, a current ratio of 3.0 means that the company's current assets, if liquidated, would be sufficient to pay for three times the company's current liabilities.

Debt ratio

A company's debt ratio is a leverage ratio: how much is owed to the company compared with how much the company owes to others. The current ratio compares only current assets and debts. The debt ratio compares total assets and total debts. When the first is divided by the second, the result shows to what degree the company's total assets have been financed by borrowing. A debt ratio of 40 per cent, for example, indicates that 40 per cent of the company's assets are based on loans.

Debt may be good or bad. It depends on what the borrowing is being used for and its cost against the potential profit. During times of economic stress or rising interest rates, companies with a high debt ratio are likely to find the going tough. By contrast, during good times, debt, particularly when interest rates are low, can enhance profitability by financing growth fairly cheaply.

Inventory turnover

An inventory turnover reflects the number of times in a year that inventories are replaced. The higher the turnover, the greater should be the profit. This ratio measures efficiency and is found by dividing the cost of goods sold by inventories. It is a ratio very dependent on the nature of the industry.

A food store chain, for example, has a much higher turnover than a commercial hoverplane manufacturer so the inventory turnover ratio, like the others used by fundamentalists, should be compared with those in the same industry.

Stock valuation models

By surveying the state of the economy, industry, and company, the fundamental analyst assesses whether the company's stock is overvalued, undervalued, or correctly valued. Different models are used for evaluating the worth of a company's stock. They include dividend models which focus on the present value of expected dividends. Earnings models look at the present value of expected earnings, and asset models concentrate on the value of the company's assets.

Fundamental factors have an important bearing on the price of a share. Furthermore to discover them only a newspaper and (unless you are a walking Einstein) perhaps a calculator are necessary - no expensive software is needed, although that expenditure can pay for itself if it comes up with the right answers.

If you are relying on fundamental factors to help you determine the future price of a share, look first at its price history or you may end up owning an undervalued stock that remains undervalued. Brokers will provide these graphs for a share in which you wish to trade.

Choice of share(s): long- or short-term

So what system will you use, if any? How can you pick the share(s) or index to buy? The decision rests primarily on whether you are in the stock market for the long- or short-term.

If the latter, then you need to pick a solid share, no light task, when around 3000 shares are listed in the UK (not to mention the huge numbers available in the US, European and other equally accessible markets). A good policy is to stick to companies with a P/E ratio of no more than five or six, or with a yield above the average.

You will probably find such a share in the FTSE 100 or the Dow 350. It needs to have some volatility to provide sufficient profit on the turn. A graph will show trends and a downturn when it looks safe to enter. Buy then, make a stop loss point to ensure that you won't lose too much, and sell as soon as you make a profit, no matter how small. Use any gain you make towards the purchase of more shares.

Holding on to one that is falling will do you no favours. 'Good' shares that 'die the death', do not always resurrect themselves. There are plenty of examples of shares, and more so since the millennium, that have dropped out of the FTSE. Some may never get back and languish in the doldrums for years.

Sainsbury and Marks & Spencer were assumed in their respective retailing sectors to have a magic touch and so they did until they got arthritis and their shares tumbled. M&S has since recovered with a new line approved by the market, but it may have to work twice as hard to make the same degree of profit.

Be wary also of 'recovery' stocks which have gone through a bad patch and are now apparently on the mend. If they do turn the corner, so will you. But the chances are small. According to Warren Buffett, "When a company with a reputation for incompetence meets a new management with a reputation for competence, it is the reputation of the company that is likely to remain intact." And that goes also for failings other than incompetence.

Long-term investors are not looking for a quick buck, so must take a different approach. They need to allot more time and care to their investment cash. Use fundamentals to help pick the right shares, and a bit of technical analysis or at least a graph of the share's recent history to pick your buying and selling prices.

Both types of investors, long-term and short-, cannot lose and may gain a great deal by following the guide lines of some of the successful investors whose lives and methods are described in the last chapter.

Summary

Fundamental analysis evaluates by various ratios and other data, whether the current price of a share correctly measures a company's worth and on this basis whether the share should be bought or sold.

Return on capital employed = (pre-tax profit x 100)/capital employed

Earnings per share = after tax profit/number of shares

Pre-tax profit margin = (pre-tax profit x 100)/turnover

debt/equity ratio = (total liabilities x 100)/ordinary funds

Interest gearing = (interest expense x 100)/operating profit

Interest cover = operating profit/interest expenses

Dividend yield = (gross dividend per share x 100)/share price

Price earnings ratio = share price/earnings per share

Dividend cover = earnings per share/gross dividend per share

Chapter 10

Company reports and accounts

*"I am a marvelous housekeeper. Every time
I leave a man, I keep his house."*
Zza Zza Gabor

Company reports

UNLIKE MILLIONAIRE investors and successful managers, ordinary shareholders have neither the time nor opportunity for listening to and talking with the marketing and production teams to discover the real low-down on a company. The nearest they can get to it is through the Company Report.

Much of what goes into that report is estimated, subjective evaluation, even downright guesswork, although accounting standards boards prevent too much exaggeration (Enron, WorldCom, Xerox and others excepted!) They also wants enough disclosure to give a reasonable picture of the business. The amount of this disclosure, often beyond the requirements of the Companies Act, can backfire.

Documents now sent to shareholders may rival, in weight at least, the epic *Gone with the Wind*. This makes the paperwork almost unintelligible to the average reader. Neither does the size of the tome prevent a company hiding incompetence, fraud or dishonesty. For clues to these, and an insight into whether the business is going over the Styx, the investor needs to look at the contents, unfortunately more exhausting than exhaustive, in the company's Annual Report. Purely as a comprehension exercise, any report will do. Unless there is something the management want to hide, they all reveal much the same information (although not the figures) in much the same phrases.

Carefully read any notes which accompany the accounts. They provide some formidable statistics along with fascinating oddments, especially those relating to salaries, bonuses and pensions of the top brass, and how that total changed during the year.

Profit and loss account

For the real nitty-gritty, ignore the first few pages of the report and go to the profit and loss account. Brackets show a loss. Heading the page is **group turnover**, basically the profit from sales of services or products. View any loss with caution, although it might be due to large spending in one area of the business such as a new product or management team, more research and development, all of which could lead to future growth. The loss might be merely a one-off cost such as arises from a demerger. That won't be repeated for some years at least, so is unlikely to figure in next year's profit and loss.

Check whether it has led to 'exceptional items' such as large bonuses paid to outgoing directors, costly redundancies, or other unusual occurrences none of which is part of the company's 'normal' business. There might be a reference to them in the notes or chairman's report.

Big firms usually pursue more than one type of business, and own 'subsidiary' companies. Income comes into or goes out of the parent company from the subsidiaries. All the figures from subsidiaries and parent are grouped together on the one page and presented as the **consolidated profit and loss account.**

Group turnover

This itemises the total costs of running the company from distribution to management, wages, research and development. Some figures need a second look. A pharmaceutical company, for example, spends a lot on research and development: is it enough, too much and what is replacing the current very successful drug when the patent shortly runs out?

Operating profit/loss arises from 'ordinary activities', which conjure up all manner of 'goings on' in and out of the firm, but are actually a prosaic list of the profit/loss on various kinds of spending and income. An allowance for depreciation is an elastic component, easily expanded or shrunk to present different pictures of the firm's prosperity or lack of it. Treat with care. If insufficient funds are not allowed for *depreciation* of buildings, equipment and so on, the profit figures will be inflated and give a misleading picture of the firm's worth.

Any **sales of fixed assets** also affect the gross profit. When they are sold for more than they cost, the profit must bear comparison with their value in the balance sheet. **Operating profit (loss)** shows the cost of sales deducted from the total turnover figure. Payment of interest on money borrowed comes further down the list, another item worth a scrutiny.

After debts, interest, taxation, dividends, sales and all the rest have been received or paid out, the important so-called (because it isn't) bottom line comes next. It is referred to as **retained profit (loss)** for the financial period and is the amount that goes into the firm to pay for future activities, past ones, dividends and profits.

If there is a loss it will have to be paid back (higher interest payments next year?) Profit is generally used to expand/consolidate the business, perhaps to increase dividends by a moiety.

Any sudden downturn in profits or sales during the last part of the year, may be hidden by good figures at the beginning. Explanations for this change may be discreetly veiled in the chairman's report.

The last paragraph has more interest for shareholders and fundamental analysts than the 'bottom line' has for auditors. It shows **earnings per share** and how they have arisen. Dividing the share price by this figure gives the historic P/E ratio, once greatly beloved by analysts and fund managers but now supplemented by a few other indicators of a company's worth.

Also mentioned are dividends per share. Have they gone up or down since last year or been passed this year (bad sign)? And how does the company's financial record compare with others in the sector? Are there any notes attached to the figures which explain, for example, why one company in the group is doing badly or an area or product is doing well. Does the chairman's report hold a clue? If anything appears odd or inconsistent, play for safety, ask questions, change your strategy or your investment.

Balance sheet

Profit and loss accounts show transactions over the financial year, a balance sheet shows the worth of a company at a particular time. In brief, the top half of the balance sheet says what the company owns, the bottom half how the capital was raised to buy it. The two groups give figures for assets (fixed and current) and liabilities (fixed and current). The 'balance' is the difference between the two taken on a particular day, like a snapshot.

Individual items are listed under different headings. The resulting 'balance sheet', including subsidiary accounts, merged with the group, are sent as a consolidated balance sheet to shareholders at the end of the financial year. They rarely bother to look at it any more than they do at the profit and loss account. Yet the balance sheet indicates many things affecting the share price: it gives an idea of the company's financial strength, shows how it is using shareholders' money; whether it is making an adequate return on capital, why it might attract a possible bidder, and provides an early warning sign of possible problems.

Some items in the balance sheet which warrant a second glance are the values of **fixed assets** like shops and fittings; factories, machinery or long-term investments. Their value reduces over a working life. The reduction is the counterpart of any depreciation charge shown in a profit and loss account. **Depreciation** is more flexible than it might seem. Much depends on timing. Companies can be overcautious or over-optimistic in their views about it and the revaluation of property.

A very low depreciation charge, for example, tends to increase profits, as it is not deducted from the profit and loss account. It may also show fixed assets as being worth more now than they actually are. But writing everything off immediately is sometimes used as a ploy by newly arrived chief executives or predators who have just taken over a company. The loss can be blamed on outgoing staff and helps to make things look better later for the incoming lot.

By contrast a company that bids for another and pays for the assets more than they are worth, may write off as **goodwill** a portion of the price. This is cut from the balance sheet although not shown in the profit and loss account and weakens the company – especially when borrowed money is used.

The final paragraph, **capital and reserves**, lists the items making up shareholders' funds. With minority equity interest, this gives the **total equity** of the group. If the company stopped trading, collected all its income, repaid all its debts and sold off all its assets, this is the amount that would be available for distribution to shareholders. The figure is pure theory with a touch of farce. Although fixed assets are usually written down by a certain percentage each year, their sales might bring in very little, particularly if they represent out of date machine tools or the original cost price is eroded by inflation.

Intangible assets like patents, royalties, etc., are particularly difficult to assess, and tangible ones like land, not much easier. Enlightenment on these issues may sometimes be found in accompanying notes or in a paragraph on accounting policy.

The balance sheet snapshot on a particular day may not be representative at all of the company's financial health for the rest of the year, but it gives more than a hint of how things are progressing, ...or not, and has to be fairly consistent with previous reports of the business.

Cash flow statement

The page given to the cash flow shows how the firm's money flows in one way (operating activities; dividends; investments) and out by another (acquisitions; dividends paid; tax and debt servicing). It is a financial survey of all the **operating** activities which make up the inflow/outflow generated by the business. Investors can see how much cash the business brought in and paid out, how much was reinvested in its future and whether a company is spending cash more rapidly than absorbing it.

Returns on investment and servicing of finance show interest earned and paid. Tax and shareholders' **dividends** are deducted and financing activities **indicate whether the company has bought or sold any** fixed assets or made other investments. Exceptional items appear separately.

The bottom line in the cash flow statement: **increase (decrease) of cash** in the period, is very important. Other things being equal, an increase shows the business is being successfully run. Unless there is a very good reason for them, large cash outflows raise questions about the efficiency of management.

Look also at **cash** in the bank or **borrowings**. The latter make a business vulnerable. If not enough money is made to pay off interest, the company may not survive. The last paragraph is the oddly worded **reconciliation of net cash flow to movement in net debt**, which sounds like a fraudster's dream scenario, but actually indicates how much cash the business brought in and paid out. It also gives the **gearing ratio**, that is the ratio of net borrowings to shareholders' funds. Without a very adequate reason, a gearing ratio over 50 per cent is not a good sign. No business can continue to operate if the only result is ever-dwindling cash reserves and a rising mountain of debt.

Auditors' report

UK Companies are legally bound to produce a set of accounts every year. These are sent out in the Company Report a few weeks before the Annual General Meeting (AGM) giving the date, venue and time of the meeting, as well as motions on which shareholders can vote, for example, a rights issue or increase of directors' fees. Also included with the accounts are reports from auditors, directors and the chairman, and the key financial items outlined above: the profit and loss account, balance sheet and cash flow statement.

The auditors are accountants who are *supposed* to look at the figures from an outsider's viewpoint and see that they are readable and intelligible. Shareholders nominally appoint them; in practice the directors are responsible. No matter how scrupulously conscientious the appointees are, they will not be overzealous in finding anything wrong when their jobs are on the line.

They check whether the company is a going concern or going down the tubes. Do the accounts represent a true and fair view of the company's past progress? Investors often accept the answers as if written on tablets of stone handed down from Mount Sinai.

Past imperfect

The published figures are those of the past, not the present state of the company. They give no prediction of its future other than perhaps by a chairman's glowing picture owing more to imagination than truth. Furthermore because accounts are prepared on a 'going concern' basis, the assets represent the worth of the business now, not the actual amount available in a break-up.

Everything cannot be checked and auditors' reports tend to be quantitative rather than qualitative. Sometimes a company departs from the usual presentation because the standard rules might mislead the reader. The report explains why the rules have been breached, but if the auditors do not accept this, they will comment as such in their report.

A full auditors' report might begin with a **Statement of the auditors** 'pursuant to section 251 of the Companies Act 1985'. It states that they 'have examined the summary financial statement set out on pages...' The following paragraph, headed **Respective responsibilities of directors and auditors**, emphasises that 'the directors are responsible for preparing the **Summary Annual Report**'.

For good measure the auditors' responsibility is spelt out 'to report to you our opinion on the consistency of the **summary financial statement** within the Summary Annual Report', with the relevant requirements of 'full annual statements and Directors' report and its compliance with…' and so on.

When you have swallowed rather than digested that information and seen that no 'inconsistencies' are revealed, you learn from the next paragraph, **Basis of opinion**, that it was made in accordance with the bulletin of the Auditing Practices Board 1995/6. Then comes the auditors' **actual Opinion**… that the financial statement complies with the applicable requirements 'of section 251 of the Companies Act 1985 and the regulations made thereunder'.

This not-quite-page-turning report, conforming with current legal and accounting requirements, leaves everybody happy (except perhaps the reader). If the company has been through a cloud and weathered the storm, there might be a comforting addendum that the financial statement 'is **unqualified** and did not contain any statement under section 237(2) of the Companies Act 1985 such as inadequate records or returns, accounts not agreeing with records and returns, or failure to obtain necessary information and explanations'.

Qualifying remarks

If the auditors do have any reservations about the accounts, they mention them in 'qualifying remarks', such as:

- uncertainty about some item,
- disagreement with the directors, for example their unmerited optimism about the company's ability to pay outstanding debts.

When the concern is not serious enough to threaten the firm's survival, the auditors write that the report is true and fair save for the specified item. If the disagreement is serious or there are other doubts about the company's records, reliability and information, the auditors are bound in conscience and law to mention them.

They may suggest how such faults can be remedied but in any case will qualify their report, possibly by saying the accounts are misleading or that they can give no opinion as to whether the accounts are true and fair. Such 'qualifying' reports are equivalent to the auditors giving themselves the sack, so are rarely made. When they are, shareholders need to move out fast, although they may already be too late.

The emphasis on the directors' responsibility for preparing the accounts sounds like a get-out clause for auditors but protects them against possible later litigation if the company goes belly up or shows evidence of fraud. Another reason for this defensive attitude is that auditors are usually covered by professional indemnity insurance. In cases of fraud, the directors who are legally responsible for running the company may have untouchable hiding holes where they can salt away any ill-gotten gains.

The Chairman's Report

(Do not be blinded by figures. Look at the text; read my lips.)

The chairman's message gets front page treatment. It can be as imaginative as a *Mills & Boon* romance because the chairman has to keep his head, even when all about him are losing theirs. A downbeat message, a bad turn of phrase, could send share prices tumbling as they did with Ratner's jewellery business after an injudicious joke from Gerald Ratner. Chairmen of large companies are usually more circumspect than the smaller ones in what they say.

The chairman begins his address with the usual salutation, *Dear Shareholder*, announces the date of the next Annual General Meeting, and reviews the progress of the past year. No matter how difficult the crises through which the company might have passed, the poor results or a suspension of dividends, the chairman always manages, like an evangelistic preacher, to offer a message of hope. His company, and every other one that has had a bad financial year, now has in place, invariably, a strong team, a good platform and will go all out to pursue its objective of enhancing shareholder value.

The Directors' Report

This report usually gives potted biographies of the Board of Directors with their names, background and date of appointment. In common with most of the annual report, this section is not the most riveting read, but occasionally gilded by photos of the directors decoratively slotted into the text. There are some notes on what the company does, highlights of the past year, and hopeful but very cursory comments about the future, carefully worded in case the projections turn out to be wrong. The directors cannot then be accused of any misrepresentation.

Investors should search the report for hidden clues on the health of the company. The extensive notes, sometimes in the end pages under the heading **Accounting policies** amplify or explain figures mentioned elsewhere. They may also comment on the source and application of funds showing where the company got its cash and how the money was used.

If any of the Board is leaving, whatever the reason (retirement, a demerger with the company being split into separate parts, etc.), questions should be asked. Is this a 'downsizing' exercise? Will the firm profit from it? Are the outgoing directors receiving a bonus or payoffs? How much? What about the ethics? The warning signs of a business in trouble usually come when sales are rising faster than profits, debtors rising faster than creditors and either rising faster than sales.

The right share choice

So having perused the company reports, what system will you use, if any? Fundamental or technical analysis of a combination of the two? Will either or both help you pick the right share(s) or index to buy? Even if you have a professional adviser, the answer to these questions is the same: guidelines that suit you personally.

As pointed out in the opening chapters of this book, you must consider your attitude to risk, investment aims, and the time available to achieve them. Systems are there only to help get the aims you want within the time frame you have, against the risks you are reasonably happy to bear.

Ask yourself again if you are in the stock market for the long or short term, for retirement or excitement. If long term, you will not be looking for a quick buck, so allot more time and care to the allocation of your investment cash. Go through company reports and use fundamentals to help choose the right shares or at least study a graph of their recent history to pick the best buying price.

The long view

When investing for retirement or a date more than ten years ahead, you need a solid growth share, no easy matter when there are around 3000 shares listed in the UK (not to mention the huge numbers available in the US, European and other equally accessible markets).

A good policy is to choose companies with a P/E ratio of no more than five or six, or a yield at least ten per cent above the average. You will probably find such a share in the FTSE 100 or the Dow 350. Lists of the top performing shares are given in most financial newspapers. A graph show trends and a downturn when it looks safe to enter. Buy then, make a stop loss point to ensure that you won't lose too much.

For those already retired and looking for income, then safety and income can be found in half a dozen well-timed gilts. Select those with different months for dividend payments. As these are paid half-yearly your choice will give you a modest monthly income. It will never rise like some spectacular shooting star into the financial firmament, but neither will it plunge to earth like a meteorite. Alternatively, try a high yielding share currently down on its luck but with a good pedigree and in an economic climate likely to restore its health.

If you are one of the increasing number of investors who take moral/ethical considerations into account with your portfolio, several firms and unit trusts operate filters to prevent investment in shares considered unsuitable. Ethical shares rarely reach the top-performing bracket, but rarely touch the bottom either and usually manage to provide their supporters with income and an easy conscience.

The short term

The risk-averse short-term investor (they do exist, liking excitement but not loss) can buy a small 'lot' of one or more shares when the market is down. It needs some volatility to provide sufficient profit on the turn. Technical analysis is likely to be of more help than the fundamental approach as it will give indications of the right time to go in and out. Sell as soon as there is a profit to be made, no matter how small. Even only $20 a day adds up in 260 days to $5200, often on a very small outlay. In three years that becomes, excluding interest, a nice little sum of $15,600.

Do not bemoan the fact that you came out too soon. Have you ever met anybody who got in at the bottom and out at the top? If so, congratulations, you have met the biggest romancer on earth. Use your gain towards the purchase of another share. Holding on to one that is falling does the short-term investor no favours.

Both types of investors, long-term and short-, cannot lose and may gain a great deal by following the guidelines of some of the successful investors whose lives and methods are described in the last chapter of this book. Before doing so, however, they are directed to the following section – the Attic Room. There they may pick up some items, which may prove valuable in volatile or depressing times.

The attic room

Big houses in England, common before an age of apartments and flat dwellers, used to have in the eaves upstairs, a space known as the attic room. Rarely used for living purposes, it was full of bric-a-brac, broken furniture, ill-judged purchases and presents, all shed like discarded lovers. They lay alongside pincushions and handkerchief sachets bought, for the sake of the vicar, at sales of work. Nearby, an old family rocking horse slept with a white elephant under a mass of jumble. Such a mêlée made wonderful story material.

A member of a later generation living in the house or a poor tenant renting a room, would, (so the story line went), venture into the attic and suddenly discover a Sisley, Vermeer, an early de Kooning or an original manuscript of Keats dumped alongside old records, and broken chairs, its value until that very minute, unrecognised. The lucky finder is thereupon pitched into fame and fortune and (money being a powerful aphrodisiac), a romantic love match.

This section of the book is akin to the attic room. There are 'finds' within it, uplifting after the dispiriting appraisal of company accounts. Like the attic room it is also full of oddments, the worth of which might similarly go ignored or unrecognised. Dusted up a little they can yield if not fame, fortune, or love, at least some useful titbits. They show events and sentiments that influence share prices; and cause them to change. The oddments can also give the average investor a head start over the crowds panning or panting for gold.

Directors' dealings

Begin your search with directors' dealings. The figure for the shares they own are given in the company's annual report, which also provides particulars of contracts or arrangements entitling them to share ownership. Newspapers update those figures. Look in their financial columns or on your favourite financial Web site (Hemscott is a good one), for further particulars.

Directors are the ultimate insiders. If they start buying shares in their own companies, climb aboard with them. The dreadful events in America when the World Trade Center was destroyed by suicide bombers in aircraft carrying innocent passengers knowing they were going to their deaths (the mind recoils at such cruelty) might have seemed the end of financial interests for years to come.

But life goes on and needs money as well as charity. Those with money can use it for whatever legal purpose they like: pleasure and enjoyment; good or evil. Money bestows power. If you can lawfully create or increase it through talent, luck, ambition, business or financial expertise without harming anyone else in the process, why not?

Shrewd investors who kept an eye on directors' dealings after that dreadful September day when terror struck America, spotted some odd trends later developing in the UK market and made a profit out of them. They noted directors paid £25 million to buy stock, and sold £12 million. The pattern continued into October, when board members made 91 purchases for £5.9 million in the first five working days against eight sales worth £1.4 million.

It does not take an Einstein to realise that when a director buys large quantities of shares in his own company, he does not expect to lose anything by doing so. Conversely, if he sells large quantities, he is obviously not hoping to make a fortune by holding them. Unless there is some cogent reason for his action (imminent retirement; sickness; emigration), investors won't do badly by following his example. The race is to the swift. Whether buying or selling, don't hang about. The corporate world doesn't. A week after the terrorist attack, the FTSE 100 index regained all its losses – and more.

Interest rates

Unlike taxes imposed on goods, interest rate changes do not immediately affect prices, except in the stock market. Rates have already been mentioned (in chapter 5) in connection with their impact on gilts. A 'real' interest rate is the nominal one adjusted for inflation, so that if a stock yields 6% and the inflation rate is 4%, the holder of the stock gets only 2%. That is the 'real' interest rate and prices adjust to fit that figure.

Interest rate changes affect all forms of credit including mortgages and ultimately house prices. But again, not immediately. This gives canny investors the chance to adjust their spending and borrowing habits to take advantage of the changes.

Academics write tomes on the Keynesian and classical theories of interest, but sufficient for the purposes of this chapter are the effects of rises and falls in interest rates on share prices. Rises tend to depress them and are usually due to (a) inflation, because lenders look for a higher return on the money they lend, or (b) a balance of payments deficit or exchange rate difficulties.

When governments think these situations are likely to happen and worsen, they have to offer higher rates to induce people to hold bonds, prevent an outflow of capital and to attract funds from abroad.

Investors should hang on to their shares and reduce their borrowing; traders stop buying on margin. The most likely beneficiaries in this situation are bank shares and others supplying the demand for capital. Building society depositors also gain as interest rates rise.

Business confidence

A fall in interest rates can stimulate business confidence if the rate seems sufficient. A quarter point may do little and need 'renewing' very shortly afterwards. The US Federal Reserve ('Fed') made nine interest cuts of this amount before October 2001 in an effort to stimulate the economy. When a reduction even of several interest rate cuts fails to stimulate the economy taxation (fiscal policy) may be used to stimulate demand.

Reduced taxation puts more money into people's pockets. So does an increase in public sector spending. Business confidence increases, more jobs are created, at first in the retail sector (food, drink, clothes), then, if the exchange rate is not too heavily weighted against them, manufacturers may try a toe in the water.

The US government and various other agencies, including the Federal Reserve, provide an immense amount of data relating to business growth, consumption, production and employment. In the UK, **cyclical indicators** of business and consumer confidence are issued monthly by the Office of National Statistics.

They monitor and predict changes in the UK economy based on various surveys and provide early indicators of **cyclical turning points** in economic activity. The Treasury also gives predictions for the UK economy and many public and private bodies provide their own forecasts. Whether long-term investors agree with them all or not, they should certainly take a look, first at the company's profits and then at this free material from government sources and others, before choosing a share.

Bids and rights

A **bid** for a company or even the rumour of a bid almost always sends a share price up, whether the company being bid for is doing OK, or is practically on its knees. It makes no difference. The bidder thinks there is a profit to be made by getting bigger, or by buying the company to break it into several parts. Investors need to get in early or not at all. Short-term investors can move in or out of the company being bid for quite profitably, but need to keep abreast of the news.

By contrast, a **rights issue** tends to depress the share price in the short term. Shareholders get the right to subscribe for extra shares in the company, based on a ratio of their holding such as one new share for every 20 held. The rights issue shares are offered at a discount to the existing share price.

Shareholders need not take the offer up or they can do so and hold, or hope to sell the new shares at a higher price in the market. As a rights issue is often made when a company needs extra cash, the chances of a quick fix depend on the strength of the company making the offer. When the issue is successful, an ailing company can sometimes regain a little strength. If the company has a good record and wants cash for expansion, the rights issue provides an opportunity for short-term investors to make a profit by selling the shares. Long-term investors can stay in for the ride.

Market movements

"No man is an island." Neither is an index. If US share prices rise, perhaps owing to a cut in interest rates by the 'Fed', it is almost certain that sooner or later, the UK stock market, and probably the European, will rise too, although the latter to a lesser extent as their shares are not usually traded so heavily.

Japan's economy is more insulated and the market tends to perform rather differently, especially since the country's interest rates were driven down to almost zero to pull the country out of its recession.

Changes in the market can also occur as a result of price movements in only one share if it is big enough. In the USA, movements in the share prices of Cisco, Microsoft, AOL, or IBM, Gillette and Coco Cola (favourites of Warren Buffett) will make the rest of the market tremble with glee or despair.

In the UK, giants like Vodaphone similarly influence the whole market, not just the sector alone, by their performance, good or bad. Short-term market movements are affected largely by crowd psychology; long-term by fundamentals such as economic and political factors.

Sector movements

These are even more pervasive. Nasdaq fluctuations affect dot-com stocks in the UK and technology stocks in Europe. When a country has a large industry, like electronics, based on one or two big players, for example, Dell computers in Ireland or Nokia mobile phones in Finland, any fall in the Nasdaq adversely affects that company specifically; the stock market, employment levels and the currency, overall. A foreign investor in Irish shares will feel the pinch of the punt.

It needs a very strong company to stand out against the crowd. The effect of a downturn in one share is also seen in the heavier manufacturing industries because companies in these sectors have numerous subcontractors. Their share prices will reflect the upturn or downturn in the company they supply.

Pharmaceuticals are another 'sympathetic' sector where bad results by one company, because of, for example, the failure of a drug at trials, the threat of or actual litigation, the end of royalties or patents, can affect the whole sector.

Retailers often weather storms of other companies in their particular sector because they have an exceptionally good product, better marketing or stricter cost control.

Crowd psychology

This topic needs a chapter, indeed a book, all to itself but is being kept under restraint in the attic room. Intangible though the concept is, the effects of crowd psychology can be seen on any graph which shows trading volume. When share prices move upwards, everybody rushes in to buy; when prices fall, everybody scrambles out of the share as fast as they can. The big motivating forces, as has been noted earlier in this book, are fear, panic and greed.

Fear arises from many causes, often difficult to identify. They range from an antipathy to spiders, a horror of rodents (read again George Orwell's wonderful book *Nineteen Eighty-Four* to get the 'feel'), to fears such as those of heights or open spaces that actually immobilise their sufferers.

Other fears may be based on actual experience of disasters like a rail crash; or destructive forces of nature which destroy crops, factories and populations. These have an impact not only on insurance firms or the industries and areas directly involved but also on spectators far removed from the disaster scene.

The attack on the World Trade Center highlights this fact. The UK tourist industry already damaged by a foot and mouth epidemic, endured another blow. Entertainment (encompassing the theatre which is very dependent on American tourists), catering and the subsidiary food industries also suffered.

Although the aircraft industries were already failing (too many routes; too many governments putting national pride before the national purse) the terror bomb accelerated their decline. Americans who use the air almost as much as the car, temporarily gave up flying. So did many fearful people who had been nowhere near the catastrophe. However, falling markets never fall in a straight line and it was possible by judicious timing to make profits even in a falling market such as British Airways temporarily suffered.

Sometimes huge market falls take place like that of Black Monday 1987 without any real cause. This rapid fall was due entirely to crowd psychology. There was no fundamental reason why the market appeared about to collapse. Fear took hold. Panic ensued.

Everybody rushed to sell. What made the situation worse was that it became impossible to contact brokers. The 'spread' seemed to be enormous and prices abysmal. Fortunately governments and institutions had learnt something from the even worse market collapse in 1929 and by the use of prudent policies staved off any lasting disaster.

With investors, fear usually arises from lack of self-confidence. The chance of losing money, especially a large sum, causes fear, and then as more people become aware of the chance of loss, panic ensues. Such a situation is easily avoided by investing not just what you can afford, but what you can afford to lose.

Economists aver profit is the reward of risk, but risk is part of life. With money as in life there are few guarantees. Even with a sure-fire win, you may not be there to receive it. Sell short if you must, but only when you know you can equably bear a subsequent loss. You will then be able to sleep easily at night and take market convolutions in your stride.

As for greed, who is not subject to it at some time? Probably only saints and those who have taken vows of poverty, ...and who knows, they may fall victim to the greed for power. Stock market greed takes the form of always wanting the last cent, the last penny, the last euro, or whatever, an attitude which causes investors to hang on too long, afraid to sell in case they miss the last drop of juice that can be squeezed out of a share.

Remember the old stock market adage of leaving something for the other fellow. It still holds more than a grain of sense.

Summary

Figures talk. Check them before you buy.

Chapter 11

Advice from the great investors

*"The danger with spending your life telling stories
about the way it treats you is that you can keep improving
the material and losing the facts."*
Basil Boothroyd

Introduction

SUCCESSFUL investors do not, as the proverb has it, 'open mouth and wait for roast duck to fly in'. All deliberately followed a course that proved right for them. And whatever the secret of successful investment, whether it be luck, knowledge, judgement or experience, or a combination of all four, certain individuals obviously have it.

The rich

Do not, however, be too impressed with tales of famous investors who made millions. Richard Branson showed how it could be done when he said, "To become a millionaire, be a billionaire and buy an airline".

Few really rich people start off dirt poor. They usually began like Bill Gates, or William Hewlett and David Packard, as young men madly keen about a new project they had dreamed up. With a little money, borrowed or earned they developed and marketed their ideas, made their first pile, then wisely invested it to make more.

A few women appear in publications listing THE RICH, such as *Forbes Magazine* in the US, or *The Rich Report* from the UK's *Mail on Sunday*. Until recently, they rarely achieved this fame by investment expertise alone, that accolade, so much envied by THE POOR.

They often started investing after marrying/divorcing rich men; or were part of a family with entrepreneurial experience: Leona Helmsley (hotels); Sydell Miller (hair products); or as fund managers like Nicola Horlick, paid highly for managing other people's money.

A few exceptional women, like Joyce C. Hall, the founder of Hallmark Cards, or Anita Roddick of Body Shop (who could not even manage to get a loan from the bank and had to go along with her husband to get it) started up their own businesses: investment came later.

Others, like Marjorie Scardino, became directors or chief executives in high profile companies (*Financial Times*) or financial institutions; like Helena Morrissey of American-owned, Newton Asset Management.

In these fields they have done extraordinarily well, even managing to have and nurture children on their way to the top. But perhaps there is only one group of women that has grown rich through investment alone in recent years, and not by becoming fund managers or entrepreneurs themselves. They are those who started buying regularly a few shares when they were young, lived to be centenarians and spent practically nothing en route. There are very few of them about.

Unlike gamblers or buyers of lottery tickets, investors are assumed to be rational people. Many are rational only when they have tried all other options. Men, in particular, tend to be overconfident in their investment decisions and ability to pick the shares that are going to zoom upwards. The Internet makes it so easy, and riskier. A click, a password, a few more clicks and you can buy/sell a parcel of shares worth hundreds, perhaps thousands of dollars, pounds, yen, francs, Deutsche Marks, or whatever. Nothing could be simpler.

Gender difference

Further, it appears men enjoy risk more than women do. They see it as a challenge, something to be overcome. Even the risk of losing money hardly daunts them, perhaps because the idea of loss rarely enters into a gambler's mentality and investing in shares without thought, knowledge or judgement is in effect a form of gambling. Academic studies emphasise that men's attitude to risk applies also to their investment strategy.

A working paper by Barber and Odean of the University of California in 1999 entitled *Boys will be Boys: Gender Overconfidence and Common Stock Investment*, made some interesting points about male and female investors.

Men traded 45 per cent more often than women and single men traded 67 per cent more often than single women. Trading does not use the buy and hold approach of investment. Instead frequent deals are made, perhaps several times in a day to get profits from shares constantly on the move. More trading means higher costs with not always higher returns. That may be why the study showed that male investors performed less well than women by one percentage point a year.

Against this somewhat dismal tale of *trading*, competitions over the past decade suggest that men are the top performers in the *investing* stakes. This may be the situation during rising markets. Judging by a 2001 UK survey of 3207 investors it does not appear so likely when share prices are falling.

The research by online financial information company DigitalLock between 1st August and 31st October 2001, incorporated the terrorist attacks on 11th September. The FTSE 100 and All Share indices fell by 22 per cent to the end of October. Against that dismal background, women made an equally dismal profit of only two per cent. The men's record was worse, their average portfolio falling by 26 per cent. More than half of them (55%) were happy to invest in volatile shares such as the dot-coms and technology companies. Only 33% of women were prepared to do so.

Professor Cary Cooper of the University of Manchester Institute of Science and Technology (School of Management), said the findings emphasised the male investor's macho attitude to life. "…they want to climb in their careers and lives and they carry that over into the shares they buy. …women…intuitively choose businesses they know are going to stay around."

Changing patterns

Whether the professor's idea of male investors is true or not, it is certainly obvious that women are becoming increasingly involved in business and investment. According to Merrill Lynch of the New York Stock Exchange, the number of women investors rose by 85% during the period 1985 to 2000. The figures, from the Investment Company Institute and the Securities Industry Association, look like the start of an expanding global trend that has witnessed a near doubling of the number of females in financial markets.

Winthrop H. Smith Jr, chairman of Merrill Lynch International and president of the firm's International Private Client Group (IPCG) thinks one reason for the rise is the growth in the number of women in the world's workforce. They have more money, more independence and better education than their grandmothers and sometimes their parents.

Another reason was that, as a matter of survival, more people want to enter financial market places. They know they can no longer rely on the pension system alone for their retirement and must take steps to safeguard their own future. The increasing level of global financial education and knowledge is, so Merrill Lynch IPCG avers, a further contributing factor to the greater interest by women in the stock markets.

Distinct differences between female and male investment habits have also been identified. Women, tend to have different economic goals and realities than male investors. This distinction means women tend to choose slightly more conservative products.

Most people invest in shares today, because other than starting up their own business or investing in real assets like property, (which need more capital as a starter plus a possible 20- or 30-year loan), share ownership can be started with as little as $500–$1000. This kind of investment is within reach of most people within a lifetime. It seems to hold out the best chance of a good lifestyle and possibly even a small fortune at some future date.

Maxims for success

In *How to be a Billionaire* by Martin S. Fridson gives 12 key principles to this financial heaven. Some are not applicable to investment and advice like *Invest in Political Influence and Resist the Unions*, are hardly mainstream, and unlikely to be readily acceptable in the UK.

However, the principle in the book of 'Buy Low', as illustrated by the life of Warren Buffett is certainly a good maxim for investors. So is the motto of Shelby Cullom Davis, a rare and remarkable investor, *"Use it up, wear it out, make do or do without"* – although this precept seems somewhat outdated in a consumer society.

At the age of 40 without any form of economics training, Davis quit his state job for the stock market and put $100,000 of his wife's money into insurance stocks. Here one can interpolate with an Irish grandmother's advice for would-be millionaires, "Don't marry for money, but marry where money is."

Cullom Davis stayed the course through booms and busts for nearly 50 years, and at his death he had built a portfolio worth nearly $900 million multiplying his original stake 18,000 times. He left his astounding fortune to a trust. To his son, Shelby Davis the second, his two grandsons, Chris and Andrew, he left the running of the family mutual funds business, one of the most successful in Wall Street history.

He also bequeathed his philosophy of working hard, playing hard, spending sparingly, and applying common sense to matters of investing. His fascinating story is told by John Rothchild in The Davis Dynasty.

Another remarkable investor, a fund of pithy comments and a legend in his own time, is Warren Buffett. Reputedly one of the world's most successful and richest investors, a glance at his life and investment principles might yield a dollar or two.

Warren Buffett

Known as the Sage of Omaha in reference to his birthplace, Warren Buffett started his investment career at eleven years old by marking the board in his father's stockbroking firm. He bought his first shares then.

Critics might say that having a stockbroker father was akin to being born with a silver spoon in his mouth. How could he not become one of the richest men in the world? But thousands of others start life with silver spoons. They soon lose their lustre. Buffett transmuted his into gold through his gift for numbers.

While a student at the University of Nebraska he came across *The Intelligent Investor*, a book written by Benjamin Graham. A Columbia University professor, the author held the view that a company's intrinsic value was the core piece of information that every investor should know. Having made this calculation, they should buy stock only when its price was below its calculated value.

Early Influences

John Maynard Keynes, in a letter to a business associate ("…there are seldom more than two or three enterprises at any given time to which I personally feel myself to put full confidence") had already given the initial idea to Buffett of focus investing. Graham's book with its mathematical approach intrigued him still further and he enrolled at

Columbia University to study under the author, then returned to Nebraska with an economics degree.

He began working in his father's firm, using Graham's investment principles, and later joined him in the Graham-Newman Corporation in New York. Two years later, Graham retired. Buffett went back to Nebraska. With seven partners and $100 of his own money he set up his own firm.

Opportunity knocks

In 1963 came the Tino de Angelis salad oil scandal. It also provided Buffett's first big opportunity (later duplicated) to try out Graham's ideas. Investors feared American Express would be held liable for millions of dollars of fraudulent warehouse receipts. Its share price dropped from $65 to $35.

Buffett invested $13 million or 40 per cent of his partnership's assets, buying in this way five per cent of the company. During the next two years, the price tripled and Buffett found himself $20 million in profit. He disbanded the firm a few years later owing to what he felt, correctly, to be dangerously high stock market valuations.

His skills in picking stocks and fee income from investment management have made him a billionaire, and created a happy band of rich investors. So what lessons can be learnt from his example and his witty pronouncements at college lectures and in annual reports?

Value or growth

Although he started out as a value investor interested chiefly in assets, he has since become a growth investor. He focuses on a few shares and holds them long term. This stance has given him a compound return of around 22.3% over 36 years.

Focusing is quite a different form of portfolio management from the other two types practised today: **active**, where managers constantly buy and sell a large number of stocks, and **passive**, such as index tracking. This involves assembling a diversified group of stocks designed to copy the behaviour of a specific benchmark or index such as the Standard & Poor's 500 or the FTSE 100.

Of these two strategies Buffett prefers the tracker. By periodically investing in an index fund its diversification strategy enables 'know nothing' investors to outperform most investment professionals.

However he diluted this advice by adding that conventional diversification made no sense for those 'know nothing' investors, who understood business economics and could find five to ten sensibly priced companies which possessed important long-term competitive advantages. As an aside one might feel these are hardly 'know nothing' investors.

Unlike the diversification practised by both active and passive investors, Buffett is a focus investor who concentrates on a few good shares.

Some of his guidelines

Shares represent part-ownership of a business. When considering their purchase think like a prospective owner. Focus on the underlying business, not the stock. What does it do? How well does it do it?

Stick to businesses you understand so that you can grasp the true value of what you own. Only a few are worth buying. Narrow your search down to those.

Act as though you have a lifetime decision card with just twenty chances on it. With every investment decision your card is punched, and you have one fewer available for the rest of your life.

Buffett thinks that great businesses possess the following characteristics:

- Simplicity: they are easily understood, straightforward to manage.
- Strong business franchises: they benefit from 'economic goodwill', that is the ability to keep raising prices above the level of inflation.
- Predictability: their earnings can confidently be projected into the future.
- High returns on capital: achieved without resorting to creative accounting or excessive debt. This is even more important than headline earnings.
- Strong cash generation: they do not require heavy reinvestment in assets but have enough cash to invest in pursuit of even greater profits.
- Devotion to shareholder value: the management has a significant amount of its own capital tied up in the business.

Discounted cash flow

He uses **discounted cash flow** (DCF) to estimate the future cash flows of the business. He discounts this calculation back to a present day value by applying the possible alternative rate of return in a benchmark bond without risk, for example, ten-year UK gilts. This shows whether there is a safe enough gap between the current and projected values of the business.

Estimate its intrinsic value: price is what you pay, value is what you get. Allow a sufficient margin of safety between the two, so that, you are in effect paying 50p or 60p for £1 of value. If your estimates err on the high side, that margin still allows for a good return. Ignore stock market gyrations.

When to sell

Sell only on one or more of the following conditions. When:
- the company's intrinsic value is not increasing at a satisfactory rate
- its market value vastly exceeds its estimated intrinsic value
- you need the cash to invest in a company that is even more attractive on the basis of the gap between its intrinsic and market values.

Quoting Benjamin Graham's dictum that "*Investment is most intelligent when it is most businesslike*", Buffett declares them to be the nine most important words ever written about investing.

His annual reports and speeches are published as *The Essays of Warren Buffett*. Robert Hagstrom's *The Warren Buffett Way* (1994) and *The Warren Buffett Portfolio* (1999) are excellent descriptions of the system as well as being enthusiastic tributes to a great investor who has become an American folk hero.

Other successful investors and their systems

A fistful of others whose lives, analyses and advice are worth reading include Philip A Fisher and his younger son Kenneth, Peter Lynch, John Neff, William J O' Neill, T. Rowe Price (who before his retirement was the head of the Baltimore investment firm he founded), Jim Slater (better known to UK investors), Sir John Templeton and Ralph Wanger. Not all of these were investors working as individuals for themselves. Some like Rowe Price, Templeton and Lynch founded or ran investment firms.

Peter Lynch

Like Warren Buffett, Peter Lynch was not afraid to give out his ideas on the right time to buy and sell. The time to buy, he suggested, was when growth stocks were out of fashion. Their P/E ratio will have fallen to roughly the same level as the market. Start buying when the P/E is about 33% higher than the lowest point it reached at the bottom of the last few cycles. Continue buying until the price starts to rise strongly above this initial level. Concentrate on industry leaders. They usually have above-average earnings growth.

Rowe Price declared that even amateur investors who lacked time and training to manage their investments could be reasonably successful if they selected the best managed companies in fertile fields for growth. Buy these shares and retain them until they can no longer be regarded as a growth stock.

When Peter Lynch took over the Fidelity Magellan fund in 1977, it was worth $22 million. By 1990 when he retired, its value was $14 billion. He became the only manager in history to run so large a fund, so successfully, for so long. During his time at Fidelity, he made an average 29% compound over 13 years and his book, *Beating the Street*, records small growth companies as his biggest successes. Among them were the 16-bagger Rogers Communication Inc., Telephone Data Systems (an 11-bagger) and Envirodyne (a ten-bagger). Also a ten-bagger was Oprah Winfrey's production company, King World Productions.

Working six and sometimes seven days a week, with a total staff of two research workers, Lynch ran at any one time, a portfolio of 1400 stocks, meeting brokers and company managers every day. He specialised mainly in growth and recovery stocks, holding them sometimes for years, sometimes for months, and admitted that half of them were mistakes.

His punishing work schedule appears very American to the English, neither easy to export, nor one that most investors would wish to copy. It seems hardly surprising that his firm became so successful and that he took early retirement to spend more time with his family.

What then can smaller investors learn from him? Any of them, he alleges, can research stocks better than most professionals, and make smarter decisions about what to buy. They are often better placed to spot potentially profitable investments early and are free to act independently, unrestrained by committees, trustees or superiors.

Rather than holding cash it is better, he suggests, to put any spare money into 'stalwarts' so that you do not miss out on rising markets. He does not define 'spare money' and emphasises ignoring the vagaries of the market by staying fully invested at all times. Personally I still prefer a bit of cash to 'stalwarts' in times of emergency. In *One Up on Wall Street*, Lynch does define the rest of his terms, by categorising companies into six main types:

- **Slow growers** – raising earnings at about the same rate as the economy, about 2–4% a year.
- **Stalwarts** – good companies with solid EPS growth of 10–12%.
- **Fast growers** – small, aggressive new companies growing 20–25% or more.
- **Cyclicals** – whose earnings rise and fall as the economy booms and busts.
- **Turnarounds** – companies with temporarily depressed earnings, but good prospects for recovery.
- **Asset plays** – companies whose shares are worth less than their assets, provided these assets could be sold off for at least book value.

He advises concentrating your efforts on finding fast growers. If bought at the right price, some of these can become ten-baggers (shares that multiply your investment ten times over). Otherwise, look for 'turnarounds' and perhaps the occasional 'asset play'.

He favours companies with a forecast P/E ratio well below their forecast EPS growth rate (i.e. a low PEG); a strong cash position, and avoids those with a high debt-to-equity ratio ('gearing'), especially if the debt takes the form of bank overdrafts, which are repayable on demand, rather than bonds, which are not.

In the case of 'stalwarts' and 'fast growers', he looks for a high pre-tax profit margin and in 'turnarounds', for a low one with the potential to rise.

When to sell

Sell when the stock is 30% above your upper buying price limit. Sell it off gradually as the price continues to advance. (Rowe Price sold 10% every time the price rose 10%. Smaller investors might perhaps sell 25–33% on each 20% advance.) Also sell if you can be reasonably certain the bull market has peaked or the company appears to be entering its mature phase, reports bad news or the stock price collapses on widespread selling.

Decisions should be made on specifics not generalities, in other words Lynch believed that profits and losses depend on factors specific to the company itself, not the economy as a whole. Again I would take issue with this: only very small companies are immune to what happens in the world about them. Profitable as they may be at any one time, if the world suddenly tumbles about their ears, they too will go down with the rest.

Buying whenever you come across an attractive idea with an attractive story behind it, which he also recommended, seems however, more in tune with current thinking. The rest of his selling philosophy can be summed up as follows:

SELL:

- **stalwarts** when their PEGs reach around 1.2–1.4, or when the long-term growth rate starts to slow
- **fast growers** when there appears to be no further scope for expansion (expansion begins to produce only disappointing sales and profits growth) or their PEGs reach around 1.5–2.0
- **asset plays** when they are taken over (assets that are sold off fetch lower than expected prices).

T Rowe Price

A cyclical investor in long-term growth companies, T. Rowe Price had a work ethic somewhat approaching the style of Peter Lynch. He never deviated from the daily agenda he set himself, or from his decisions about when to buy and sell stocks. He demanded the same discipline from his employees, a style which made his firm one of the largest asset managers of his day.

Initially buying at the bottom of the business cycle and selling at the top, he later switched to a more value-driven style and invested in steady growth, oil and gold stocks. He defined growth stocks as shares in business enterprises with favourable underlying long-term growth in earnings. They also had to show possibilities of future continued growth over several business cycles. Furthermore, earnings should reach new high levels at the peak of each subsequent major business cycle.

Rowe Price was perhaps more of an entrepreneur than a manager often starting a fund and then after its establishment, moving on to launch another one. Some of his most famous funds are still running today. The sample family portfolio which he published showed how he turned $1000 invested in 1934 into $271,201 by the end of 1972 – a compound return of about 15.4% over 39 years.

When to buy

His advice on when to buy was first to look for leaders of companies in the earliest identifiable phase of growth, then buy when growth stocks are out of fashion and the group P/E ratio has fallen to roughly the same level as the market.

Start when the P/E is about 33% higher than the lowest point reached at the bottom of the last few cycles. Continue buying until the price starts to rise strongly above this initial level.

Rowe Price added that even amateur investors who lacked training and time to manage their investments could be reasonably successful if they selected the best managed companies in fertile fields for growth, bought and retained their shares until they were no longer 'growth' stocks.

When to sell

Rowe Price advised selling when:
- the stock is 30% above your upper buying price limit
- the company reports bad news
- the stock price collapses on widespread selling
- you can be reasonably certain the bull market has peaked and the company appears to be entering its mature phase
- on each 20% advance, small investors might consider selling at 25–33% (Price himself sold 10% every time the price rose 10%).

For more information on his life and style, read his profile in John Train's book, *The Money Masters*. *The Investor's Anthology*, edited by Charles Ellis, also has an extract 'Picking Growth Stocks' which gives Rowe Price's own views on the subject.

Sir John Templeton

At the outbreak of Second World War, Sir John Templeton made a 'killing' not on the battlefield but in finance. He did it by buying into all the 104 US stocks that were selling for less than $1. To do so, he borrowed $10,000 from his brokerage firm boss, who must have been unusually trusting, gullible or far-sighted. Ordinary investors should never rely on meeting such a combination in their own lifetimes.

The shares which Templeton bought rose to a value of $40,000 over four years and he was firmly on his way to the top. His investment style and progress were different from most other financially brilliant minds for he started again at the age of 56. At that age many people are already looking forward, although not always with relish, to their retirement years.

Sir John had different ideas. Starting a single fund, the Templeton Growth Fund, he cleverly based it at Nassau in the Bahamas. The fund became the top performer among US funds over the following 20 years. Even more noteworthy was that it showed the opportunities, not previously recognised, of spotting before the crowd, opportunities abroad. Others followed a similar route in Japan in the 1960s, and Canadian property in the 1970s.

From 1945–2000 the Templeton Growth Fund averaged gains of around 15 per cent a year. As a fundamentalist, he looked at a company's P/E ratio compared with others in the sector, its liquidity value, operating profit margins, and average growth rate, avoiding those growing 'suspiciously' fast.

Maxims for investment

The ten rules he followed for success, still used by his firm are:

- invest for real returns so as to get the maximum after taxes
- keep an open mind; stay flexible and sceptical
- don't follow the crowd; buy when others sell and sell when they buy (although this stance needs patience and fortitude)
- remember everything changes: bear and bull markets are both temporary
- avoid the popular
- learn from your mistakes
- buy during market pessimism, sell during market optimism

- hunt for value and bargains
- search world wide for more and better bargains
- no one knows everything.

William O'Neill

Although William O'Neill made a personal fortune from investment, he is perhaps as famous for his best selling book *How To Make Money In Stocks*, for his databases and his CANSLIM approach ('winning' system in good times or bad). Like Jim Slater, (whose history follows later in the chapter) he relies on a mix of qualitative and quantitative criteria to pick stocks.

Opportunity knocks

His initial success was due, unusually, to choosing stocks setting new highs – 'breaking out' might be the technical analyst's term. Using data-based stock selection that he devised himself, he was able to turn $5 into $200,000, although he has had his ups and downs. He has since gone on to create the *Investors' Business Daily* a newspaper meant to rival the Wall Street Journal and with its unique data tables, it possibly does.

He advises a rather difficult rule for investors to follow: pick out growth stocks poised for a swift price rise before you buy them. More details of his investment strategy and performance, including his famous CANSLIM approach are given in chapter 7.

Philip Fisher

An ultra long-term buy and hold investor in technology growth stocks, Philip Fisher's choice of 40 years ago is hardly flavour of the month for today's hot tipster. When he began, however, the name Silicon Valley was never even thought of. It existed only in young men's visions.

After training as an analyst in a San Francisco bank, Philip Fisher started his own investment advisory business in 1931, specialising in the type of firm for which California is best known: innovative technology companies driven by research and development. These went through the Slough of Despond in 2000–2001, but some at least could bubble up in the not too distant future.

Buying well-researched shares has helped Fisher to spot value before the crowd. He also has an unconventional and 'contrarian' approach. Not all of his advice seems practicable for ordinary investors. They cannot visit company sites and do the research of fund managers and their teams as he recommended and did himself, but some of his easier guidelines are set out below:

- concentrate your attention and your cash on young growth stocks, to identify promising prospects
- read everything you can lay your hands on
- interview those in the know (managers, employees, suppliers, customers and competitors), visit various company sites if you can, and not just the headquarters.

Advice on buying

Fisher suggests that before you buy, get satisfactory answers to some key questions. The following is a summary:

- Do the company's products or services have enough market potential for several years' sizeable sales increase?
- When the current growth potential of attractive products has dimmed, will the management develop others to increase total sales potential?
- How effective are the company's research and development in relation to its size?
- Does it have an above average sales organisation and worthwhile profit margins? What is it doing to maintain or improve them?
- Does the company have outstanding labour, executive and personnel relations and depth to its management?
- How good are the company's cost analysis and accounting controls?
- Are there other aspects of the business, peculiar to the industry, which show the investor the merits of the company relative to its competition?
- Does the company have a short-range or a long-range outlook in regard to profits?
- What about future equity financing? Will the company's growth require so much that the larger number of shares then

outstanding will cancel most of the existing stockholders' benefit from this anticipated growth?

● Is the management of unquestionable integrity and how open is it with investors, in good times and bad?

When to sell

If the job has been correctly done when a common stock is purchased, the time to sell it is – almost never – but there are three reasons when it can be considered. When:

● you have made a serious mistake in your assessment of the company
● it no longer passes the key questions as clearly as it did before
● you can reinvest your money in another, far more attractive company.

Fisher's philosophy is epitomised in the following comments: "I don't want a lot of good investments; I want a few outstanding ones." "The greatest investment reward comes to those who by good luck or good sense find the occasional company that over the years can grow in sales and profits far more than industry as a whole."

He outlined his views and methods in the book *Common Stocks and Uncommon Profits...*, and in two shorter pieces, *Conservative Investors Sleep Well* and *Developing an Investment Philosophy*. The last gives a revealing account of his early experiences.

John Neff

As a fund manager of The Vanguard Windsor Fund (Chicago), John Neff was highly regarded by professionals, many of whom trusted their money into his safe hands. They were obviously right to do so because his fund featured in the top five per cent of all US mutual funds for more than 30 years. During his 32 year tenure, the average annual total return from the Windsor Fund was 13.7% against the S&P 500 index of 10.6%.

His style was to buy good companies temporarily out of favour, with high dividends and moderate growth, selling them as soon as they rose to what he considered fair value.

Early influences

Like Buffett, John Neff was also attracted by the writing of Benjamin Graham, and applied the ideas derived from it to three equity and income funds, with spectacular results. His memoirs are now giving him the wider recognition he deserves. An early success was his investment in Ford in 1984 when the P/E ratio was 2.5 and he paid an average price for the shares of under $14. Three years later, the price was £50 and Neff had made profits for the Windsor fund of $500 million.

He is a low price/earnings investor, hunting for stock cheaply priced in relation to the total return. This is defined as earnings growth plus dividend yield, in other words, a combined growth and yield P/E ratio. He recommends comparing this ratio on your stocks and portfolio with that on the market.

He suggested avoiding stocks which significantly reduced the overall attractiveness of your portfolio. Instead set a target buying price that represents the GYP (growth and yield) you are after. Wait for the price to fall to that level. Following these recommendations, which company would you choose from these two - Company A that offers a prospective 14% earnings growth, but no dividend or Company B that has 7% growth plus a 7% dividend?

According to Neff, Company B is the better of the two, because the dividend makes the outcome more certain.

My addendum is that investors will have to judge the choice in the light of taxation and legislation in their own country.

Stock selection

Neff's criteria for choosing stock can be summed up as follows:
- low P/E ratio
- solid and ideally rising dividend
- a better than average total return in relation to the P/E ratio
- no exposure to cyclical downturns without a compensatory low P/E
- solid companies in growing fields
- a strong fundamental case for investment.

He strongly advises against chasing up highly respected growth stocks as their P/E ratios are invariably pushed up to ridiculously expensive levels creating the risk of a share price collapse.

When to sell

His criteria for selling are as follows:
- if fundamentals deteriorate
- the price approaches or matches your expectations
- immediately, if the main fundamentals of earning estimates and five-year growth rates start to slip.

His book, *Investing*, illustrates his ideas. Investors looking for company 'new lows' will find them in the back pages of the *Financial Times*.

Ralph Wanger

The investment style of portfolio manager, Ralph Wanger may seem appropriate to today's investors as he specialises in theme driven small growth companies for the medium to long term. Using this as his approach, he turned the Acorn Fund into one of the top performing funds of the last thirty years.

Yet shortly after its launch, disaster struck. The fund lost one third of its value during a market downturn. Some months afterwards, the market bounced back. The ailing fund survived. From this experience, Wanger has learnt to take fairly light-heartedly the vagaries of the stock market. His annual returns between 1970 and 1998 were 17.2% against the S&P index of 14.4%.

Through a glass brightly

Wanger has made many gains from looking at unglamorous small companies, for example, International Game Technology, the world's leading maker of slot machines. He paid $1 a share in 1988 and five years later the price rose to $40.

Investment philosophy

His philosophy is very simple: when thinking of investing, start by looking round for trends that will last for at least four to five years. His own choices focussed on:
- the information revolution and its impact on costs
- the explosion of world telephone and data networks

- leisure activities, especially when fuelled by rich, now older, baby-boomers
- outsourcing, as companies strip down to their core functions
- money management, essential for the future wealth of an ageing world
- thinking small (for the UK this means companies with a capitalisation of around £30 million – £250 million).

He gives further ideas for picking good small companies and says the best have the following characteristics:
- growing markets for their products
- good design
- efficient, low cost manufacturing
- skilled marketing
- outstanding entrepreneurial management
- high profit margins.

By contrast with T. Rowe Price, who concentrated on growth stock leaders, Wanger went further down to the industries that benefited from those leaders, an idea that can be easily copied and often brings higher and less risky rewards. This is epitomised by prospectors who went for the gold seams in Alaska and Australia, but where those who sold picks and shovels (and in Australia, water) came off best.

Although he picked small stocks for his fund, Wanger was at heart a fundamentalist. He watched the financial strength of a company, checking its balance sheet to see whether there was too much or rising debt, and what other liabilities there were, including pension payments.

He wanted real cash generation and usually avoided turnarounds, start ups and new issues. Like Jim Slater, he used the PEG as a crude measure of potential. However, he thought it better to estimate the likely earnings per share two years ahead, and to multiply them by the likely P/E in order to arrive at a probable value. Rates are higher, he points out, when interest rates are lower and vice versa.

How and when to sell

Only reluctantly.

If the right research has been done, it should be possible to hold stocks for at least four to five years until the trend plays out.

Wanger has achieved fame in another sphere other than stock picking; that is by his amusing quarterly reports. He says that some people took shares in his fund just to get the reports. His book, *A Zebra in Lion Country*, describes his experiences as manager while extracts from his quarterly reports and a profile appear in John Train's *The Money Masters*.

Kenneth L. Fisher

Like Warren Buffett, Kenneth L. Fisher was born with the proverbial silver spoon, being the son of Philip Fisher, founder manager of the investment firm bearing his name. After graduation, Kenneth Fisher worked with his father for a year, accompanying him on his research expeditions. Then, as is the way of younger sons wanting to do their own thing, he set up his own investment firm, although still keeping the research expeditions going.

Not unnaturally too, his investment style of somewhat 'contrarian' views differed greatly from that of his father. Kenneth Fisher looked for shares that had a worse image than he thought they deserved and consequently were 'dirt cheap'.

Far from discarding his father's expertise in technology shares however, he used that knowledge to good effect. As an example, in the years before high tech shares came tumbling down faster than Humpty Dumpty, he bought 1.5% of shares in a company producing computer disks. Its reputation in management and finance was poor, and publicised widely as likely to lose out to its rivals. Two years after Fisher's purchase, the price rose from the $3.50 Fisher paid, to over $55 a share.

Most investors can tell similar tales of brilliant hits, although not quite of the same order of magnitude. What is different about Fisher and other successful investors is that he also knew when to sell. He made 1500 per cent on his outlay in the year 1999 when high tech and dot-com shares were flying to the stars. Huge profits could also have been made by other investors in the same sector. Most of them missed out, ruing their 'bad luck' in the second half of the year. The outlook was even worse in the year following.

Fisher advises buying into 'super companies', that is businesses which generate naturally financed growth at above average rates. Characteristics of a 'super company' are:

- Management's zeal for growth copied by staff.
- Excellent marketing, identifying and satisfying customer needs.
- An unfair advantage, for example, being the lowest cost producer in a sector.
- Good personnel relations including listening to staff.
- Excellent financial controls.

In his book, *Super Stocks*, Fisher mentions the difficulty of evaluating loss-making stocks and offers a solution with his equation of price sales ratio (PSR). This is the division of market capitalisation by total sales. He is as devoted to this concept of the PSR as are Jim Slater and his followers (and to a limited extent Rowe Price) to their PEG calculation.

Fisher suggests that if you can find a 'super company' temporarily not doing too well with a low PSR, there is every chance it might triple in value in the next three to ten years and could even become that desideratum so often sought, so rarely found, of a ten bagger.

For safety, he adds another check on super stocks, the Price Research Ratio (PRR). This takes research and development into consideration. It is a method of assessing whether product development is cheap enough to lead to good profits. Large companies will obviously have higher PRRs (around 1.0 or more) than small ones, but the largest profits tend to come from low PRRs.

Advice on buying

His advice on buying is:
- avoid stocks with PSRs greater than 1.5
- never buy stocks with a PSR greater than 3
- search for 'super companies' with a PSR of 0.75 or less
- never buy a 'super company' selling at a PRR greater than 15
- find 'super companies' with a PRR of 5–10.

When to sell

He had only limited advice on selling, namely to sell stock in any 'super company' when the PSR goes over 3.0 or when it ceases to have the characteristics of a 'super company'.

Jim Slater

A successful investor through his picking of growth stocks at a reasonable price (GARP), Jim Slater has two other claims to fame. One, that he survived bankruptcy and came out relatively unscathed. Two, that he has popularised the PEG financial ratio (Price Earnings Growth Ratio) which is thought to have been devised in America and is now in constant use by investment analysts worldwide.

His monthly publication, *Company REFS* (Really Essential Financial Statistics), lists PEGs, other key ratios and information on UK companies. He also has a newsletter, *Investing For Growth*. Although, perhaps, more of an example to entrepreneurs than investors, his emphasis on specialising has something in common with Warren Buffett's focus investing. Slater's financial history will also be of encouragement to anybody struggling to escape from the red and into the black.

Beginnings

Jim Slater first came into an unwelcome prominence as chairman of the Slater Walker Group set up jointly with Peter Walker. Its aggressive acquisitions were not welcomed by companies or workforces drawn into their net and when Slater Walker collapsed during the 1973 recession, the resultant murmurs were hardly sympathetic. Both men fought their way out of this 'glitch', Walker going into politics and doing an excellent job in bringing some semblance of prosperity to a depressed area of Wales, while Slater went on to success through private property deals, and writing for small investors.

His book, *The Zulu Principle*, encapsulated and popularised a very simple idea, that of specialisation. As an example you study geography. Who cares? There are millions like you, who know a bit about the world. You are a nobody. Then you focus your study on one country, say Africa. You go up a notch. Now, you are something of a specialist. Anybody wanting to know about Africa comes to you.

The next step is to narrow down your specialism further still, reading and studying more and more about less and less, say the Zulus and their land in Africa. Now you are an even greater specialist, a real academic no less, approached by moguls, screen directors, or anybody whenever a situation or question arises in relation to the Zulus.

Slater suggests a similar ploy for investors, that is, to concentrate on growth shares and only growth shares. In his book, he writes that "the upside is unlimited and if the right companies are picked, the shares can be held for many years during which they should multiply the original stake many times".

Guidelines

He advises reliance on figures and financial ratios rather than qualitative judgement. (As a trained accountant, he would, wouldn't he?) The most important of these 'fundamentals' include:

- a prospective P/E ratio of not more than 20
- a prospective PEG of 0.75 or lower
- a strong cash flow
- a cash flow per share in excess of earnings per share (EPS) for the last reported year and for the average of the previous five years
- low gearing under 50%, or, better still, positive cash balances
- high relative strength in the previous 12 months, and in the preceding month or 3 months, that is, a share price which has risen further than the All Share Index in percentage terms over the same period
- a strong competitive advantage
- no active selling of shares by a cluster of directors.

What and when to buy

The best shares to buy are those with high forecast earnings growth and a low prospective P/E, that is, a low PEG. A fair value is reckoned to be when the PEG is 1.0, so search for shares with PEGs no higher than 0.75. Ideally 0.66 or lower.

When to sell

He recommends selling when:

- the prospective PEG reaches 1.2 or higher
- the calculations which caused you to buy, no longer apply
- a better opportunity presents itself.

> *"Investment is the art of the specific and selection*
> *is more important than timing."*
> **Jim Slater**

Finally: a word of caution

All the investors whose philosophy and systems have been briefly described above knew their aims, and how to get them. Having done so, they moved on. They did not buy the fashion of the moment when the price reached some spectacular height and sell when it spiralled downwards.

This, however, was the technique adopted by experienced and beginner investors alike with the new technology companies that sprouted from the end of the old century and died the death in the beginning of the new one.

Yet according to the report, *Beyond the Internet Bubble* (, by Dr Sandy Nairn (chief investment officer of the Scottish Widows Investment Partnership and former director of global equity research at Templeton Investment Management) only those with strict investment disciplines, are likely to gain from technology companies over the long term.

His previous employer, Sir John Templeton, describes the report with its subsidiary title, *Timeless Investment Lessons From 200 Years Of New Economy*, as "an important and invaluable study for investors". It gives a detailed historical survey of the interaction between new technologies and the stock market, up to and including the Internet market bubble that peaked in March 2000.

Dr Nairn traces the history of ten distinct time periods during which potentially transforming new technology was introduced and taken up with huge enthusiasm by the stock market. These technologies include the railways in the UK, railroads in the USA, the car, electric light, crude oil, the radio, the telephone, the computer and the PC.

He compares these episodes with the recent history of the Internet from its earliest beginnings in US academic and defence establishments until its emergence as a stock market phenomenon in the 1990s, culminating in the market bubble of early 2000.

His conclusions are that:

- investing in quoted new technology companies can be highly profitable for those with specialist knowledge or who move nimbly in and out of speculative bubbles before they burst, but
- it is a high risk losers' game,
- the majority of investors fail to capture the gains that are theoretically available,
- many of the companies that attract investors' capital, fail to deliver the high returns promised or expected,

- all market bubbles linked to new technology end in an oversupply of capital, and
- most of the companies set up to exploit a new technology are wiped out and periods of cutting back and recession follow.

The timing of stock market bubbles which follow the advent of new technologies usually has more to do with the economic and market conditions of the time than the technology itself. In the 2000 bubble, the quality press issued warnings about the dangers of speculative stocks, emphasising that telecom share prices were hugely overvalued. Investors ignored them and abandoned conventional wisdom. Unable (and unwilling) to apply normal valuation techniques, they succumbed to *le dernier cri* and its heavy-handed hype.

Yet even successful firms often fail to make the hoped for returns. When the new technology ceases to be a market fad, most investors lose interest in them. There are survivors: companies which enjoy some form of monopoly protection, such as patents, other legal protection or cost advantages. They provide the opportunity for profit. So do companies which can change over to electronic, instead of physical, delivery of goods and services. They might do well in the longer term. Financial services are likely to be radically transformed and many others could find it difficult to exploit the new technology.

Dr Nairn concludes by warning that those without specialist knowledge of technology should exercise patience and watch events unfold before picking the correct time to invest. "This will be when the risk/reward profile is at its most attractive, not when everyone else is clamouring to buy the same things."

So there's the warning, …and the hope.

Summary

The techniques and profiles of successful investors have many lessons for others. Learning and using them, is another story.

The last word

You've got to the end. Congratulations. What now? Remember the following:

- No system of investing works at all times.

- A system that works perfectly for one person can be a complete flop when tried by another. Ten investors could start with the same shares and the same capital and at the end of a given period, the gain and losses would be totally different. Money management is the reason.

- Learn to love your losses. Use a 15% stop loss and when you are 'stopped out' take your spouse/partner out to dinner. Celebrate the decision to take only a loss of 15% instead of 100% of capital. This way you will always be in the game and can live to fight another day.

- If you **cannot** take a **stop loss**, stay out of the market.

- Finally, your success is in your own hands. This is the FUN (yes, fun!) of investing. **If it is not fun for you, stay out of the market.**